W9-DCZ-993

DK 171.5 .T47 1985

Thomson, Gladys Scott.

C   the Great and the

NEW ENGLAND INSTITUTE
OF TECHNOLOGY
LEARNING RESOURCES CENTER

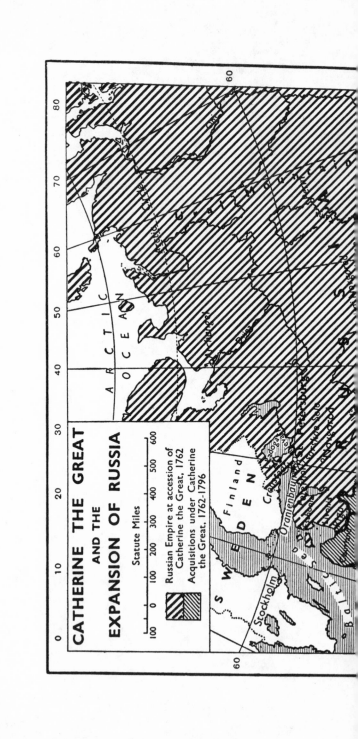

CATHERINE THE GREAT
AND THE
EXPANSION OF RUSSIA

Statute Miles

Russian Empire at accession of
Catherine the Great, 1762
Acquisitions under Catherine
the Great, 1762-1796

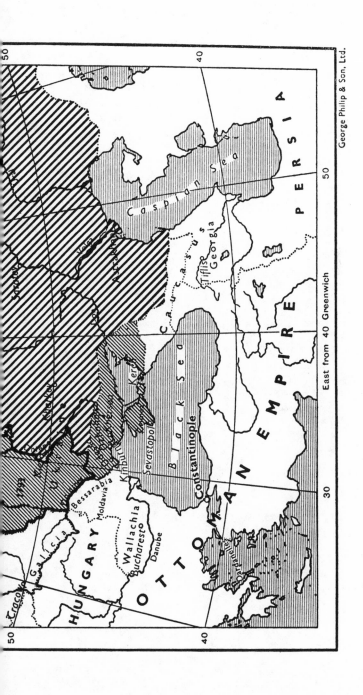

HUNGARY

Cracow

Galicia

Bessarabia

Moldavia

Wallachia

Bucharesto

Danube

Dniester

Kinburn

Sevastopol

Kerch

Black Sea

Constantinople

Dardanelles

Caucasus

Tiflis

Georgia

Caspian Sea

Volga

OTTOMAN EMPIRE

PERSIA

50

40

50

50

40

30

50

40

East from 40 Greenwich

George Philip & Son, Ltd.

CATHERINE THE GREAT

and the

Expansion of Russia

is one of the volumes
in the
TEACH YOURSELF HISTORY
LIBRARY

Edited by A. L. ROWSE

Teach Yourself History

VOLUMES READY OR IN PREPARATION

Catherine The Great
and the
Expansion of Russia

by
GLADYS SCOTT THOMSON

GREENWOOD PRESS, PUBLISHERS
WESTPORT, CONNECTICUT

7-95

#11468599

Library of Congress Cataloging in Publication Data

Thomson, Gladys Scott.
  Catherine the Great and the expansion of Russia.

  Reprint. Originally published: London : Published by
Hodder & Stoughton for the English Universities
Press, 1947.
  Bibliography: p.
  Includes index.
  1. Soviet Union—History—Catherine II, 1762–1796.
2. Soviet Union—Territorial expansion. 3. Catherine II,
Empress of Russia, 1729–1796. I. Title.
DK171.5.T47 1985   947.063   84–25245
ISBN 0–313–24748–X (lib. bdg.)

All rights reserved

Reprinted in 1985 by Greenwood Press
A division of Congressional Information Service, Inc.
88 Post Road West, Westport, Connecticut 06881

Printed in the United States of America

10 9 8 7 6 5 4 3 2 1

A General Introduction to the Series

THIS series has been undertaken in the conviction that there can be no subject of study more important than history. Great as have been the conquests of natural science in our time —such that many think of ours as a scientific age *par excellence*—it is even more urgent and necessary that advances should be made in the social sciences, if we are to gain control of the forces of nature loosed upon us. The bed out of which all the social sciences spring is history; there they find, in greater or lesser degree, subject-matter and material, verification or contradiction.

There is no end to what we can learn from history, if only we would, for it is coterminous with life. Its special field is the life of man in society, and at every point we can learn vicariously from the experience of others before us in history.

To take one point only—the understanding of politics: how can we hope to understand the world of affairs around us if we do not know how it came to be what it is? How to understand Germany, or Soviet Russia, or the United States —or ourselves, without knowing something of their history?

There is no subject that is more useful, or indeed indispensable.

Some evidence of the growing awareness of this may be seen in the immense increase in the interest of the reading public in history, and the much larger place the subject has come to take in education in our time.

This series has been planned to meet the needs and demands of a very wide public and of education—they are indeed the same. I am convinced that the most congenial, as well as the most concrete and practical, approach to history is the biographical, through the lives of the great men whose actions have been so much part of history, and whose careers in turn have been so moulded and formed by events.

The key-idea of this series, and what distinguishes it from any other that has appeared, is the intention by way of a biography of a great man to open up a significant historical theme; for example, Cromwell and the Puritan Revolution, or Lenin and the Russian Revolution.

My hope is, in the end, as the series fills out and completes itself, by a sufficient number of biographies to cover whole periods and subjects in that way. To give you the history of the United States, for example, or the British Empire or France, *via* a number of biographies of their leading historical figures.

That should be something new, as well as convenient and practical, in education.

GENERAL INTRODUCTION

I need hardly say that I am a strong believer in people with good academic standards writing once more for the general reading public, and of the public being given the best that the universities can provide. From this point of view this series is intended to bring the university into the homes of the people.

A. L. ROWSE.

ALL SOULS COLLEGE,
 OXFORD.

Contents

Introductory Note

THIS study of Catherine the Great has no pretensions to original research. It is merely an attempt to give the reader an outline of the story of the Empress and the Russia over which she ruled. References to the material from which the story is chiefly derived will be found in the text. A list of books suggested as starting-points for further study is given at the end of the volume.

My obligations to the many who have helped me are deep. In particular I would thank Dr. David Horne for the time and care given to reading the book in manuscript: and Dr. M. G. Jones for her generosity in allowing me to use her transcripts of the Report of the Commission sent by Catherine to investigate the system of education in the British Isles. I cannot easily express my appreciation of the privilege of learning first-hand from the late Sir John Hanbury-Williams accounts of the Russia in which he, like his ancestor, served: and of his kindness in allowing me to have and reproduce the photograph of the painting which appears as the frontispiece of this volume.

GLADYS SCOTT THOMSON.

Chapter One

Prologue

IN the first days of the year 1744, the fourth
year of the war known as the War of the
Austrian Succession, a girl of fifteen was about to
set out from her home in Stettin in Pomerania on
a journey to Russia. She was Sophie Auguste
Frederika, one of the two surviving children—
the other was a boy—of a petty German prince,
Christian August of Anhalt-Zerbst, governor of
Stettin, and his wife, the Princess Johanna
Elizabeth of Holstein-Gottorp.

At Stettin, the town at the mouth of the Oder,
which, after a varied history, had been ceded to
Prussia by Sweden some twenty years earlier,
Sophie Auguste had been born in the year 1729,
the month being either April or May. The place
of her birth was what was afterwards described
as a dull, grey house in the Domstrasse, but a
little later her father had become governor of the
town, and had gone to live in the Residence.
There the child grew up, against the background
of a petty German court, strictly Lutheran in its
outlook. On the whole, such a court could
probably contrive to be as dull, as disciplined in
all small matters, and as rigid as any court could

well be. There were compensations. Education, of the kind approved by the authorities, had its place in the life of the daughter of the house; a greater boon was the fact that her mother, a lively lady with a number of connections among various royal families, was fond of making visits and travelling, and her daughter was often allowed to accompany her. But the expedition on which the girl was now about to embark—and here, too, she was to have her mother's company—was to go beyond anything she had previously experienced, or had been foreshadowed in her short life.

The journey was being undertaken in consequence of an invitation from the Empress Elizabeth of Russia, and, as such invitations are apt to be, this one was in effect a command. The Princess of Anhalt-Zerbst was desired by the Empress of Russia to bring her daughter to the Russian court for a prolonged stay. The object of the invitation was not clearly defined, although secrecy was emphatically enjoined, but the father and mother, and—according to her own memoirs, written many years after—Sophie herself, must have had a fairly good idea what was in the mind of the Empress, more particularly seeing that some six months back the latter had asked for, and received, a portrait of the young girl. It was all according to custom, and no particular astuteness was needed to perceive that the purpose of the Empress was a marriage.

Elizabeth of Russia, daughter of Peter called

2

the Great, but by no means his direct successor, had now been on the throne for almost exactly three years. No more than sixteen years separated the death of her father in 1725 from her own elevation, in January of 1741, to the throne. But in that space of time the crown of Russia had passed to four sovereigns, amid vicissitudes which in some sort represented an adumbration of the twenty-nine years of turmoil which had preceded the seizure of power by Peter.

Peter's only son, the child of his first wife, had been disposed of that dreadful night in November of the year 1718, when the father had gone to the Kremlin where the young man was confined; and the next day Russia had learned that the prince was no more. He had, however, left a child, a son. And Peter, by his second wife, a peasant girl from Lithuania, had two daughters.

Four years later, in 1722, Peter had issued his edict that henceforward the ruler of Russia should nominate his successor. But he had never carried out his intention, for he had died while giving his last instructions, and before he could make clear to the daughter who was acting as his amanuensis the name he desired to be put on the paper.

The confusion which had followed had given a powerful military and political group their chance. They had placed Peter's widow on the throne. She, who was to appear in the dynastic roll as Catherine I, had lived for only two years after her accession. After her the little boy, child

3

of the prince who had died in the Kremlin, had, in his turn, been declared ruler of Russia. But within three years he had died of smallpox, and with him the male line of Romanov came to its end. There remained Peter's daughters. They, however, were not the sole representatives of the female line.

Peter had had a step-brother, older than himself, who had once shared the throne with him. This step-brother had also had two daughters; and, on the death of the boy king, it was for one of these, the younger, Anne, Duchess of Courland, that the succession had been secured. And Anne had reigned, not unsuccessfully, until her death in 1740. Before her death she had named as her successor a few-months-old child, Ivan, grandson of her elder sister. So she had thought the succession safe for her branch of the Romanov line. Peter's second daughter, Elizabeth, thought otherwise. Within a year of Anne's death, supported by the regiment of which she was the commander, she had successfully snatched the throne of Russia from the child who had succeeded as Ivan VI, sending that babe of a year old to prison, and dismissing his mother, who had been acting as regent, to a convent.

That was three years since; Elizabeth was now, in 1744, in her early thirties, reigning alone, without a consort. Alliances had, it goes without saying, been considered. Her father had contemplated marrying her to the prince who was

4

now Louis XV. The Jacobites in Scotland would, it was said, have welcomed her as a bride for Prince Charles Edward, although she had the advantage of him in years. These and other plans had come to nothing. But once there had been a betrothal. She had expected to marry a member of the Holstein-Gottorp family, Charles, brother to Johanna, wife of the governor of Stettin. The bridegroom-to-be had, however, died of smallpox before the wedding day. After this there had been lovers; even perhaps a marriage ceremony gone through with a Cossack peasant, whose voice had carried him from the steppes, where his father had been a shepherd, to the choir of the imperial chapel, and to the notice of the Empress.

Whatever the character of the ceremony, if any, this was no recognized marriage; and an Empress must have an heir. Elizabeth had chosen hers. She had a nephew, the orphaned son of her elder sister, who had married the ducal head of the Holstein-Gottorp family, cousin to the former betrothed of the Empress, and to Johanna. The boy, Charles Peter, had been brought to Russia to be subject to Russian influence; to be received into the Orthodox Church; and to be recognized as heir to the throne. Now, at sixteen years of age, he had had found for him a girl, not of Russian nationality, who was to be his wife.

Before this, there had been thought of, for a

possible betrothal, a daughter of George II of England, and also a French princess. But at the close of 1743 the Empress had made up her mind. It was the fifteen-year-old daughter of an insignificant prince of Pomerania upon whom her choice had finally fallen; and the letter had gone to Stettin.

Of the three persons at the court at Stettin who were concerned in the matter, it was perhaps the mother, Johanna, who felt the most pleasure. To her liveliness and love of travel, that lady added ambition hardly to be satisfied at a small court; and a desire to play her part in affairs, which might not unfairly be said to amount to a taste for intrigue. She could scarcely have failed to see in the letter of invitation, which had arrived while the family were spending the New Year away from Stettin with relatives, an opportunity for herself, no less than for her daughter; and it was an opportunity that might well have derived to a certain extent from her own connection with the Empress, a gratifying reflection.

But other issues were at stake; other persons were interested in Russia, and in the choice of a wife for the boy who was recognized as heir to the throne of that country.

In the course of the year 1740, the year before Elizabeth had secured the throne of Russia, two other dynastic changes had taken place in Europe. In the spring of 1740 Frederick, afterwards to be surnamed, as Peter had been, the Great, had succeeded to the throne of Prussia. In the autumn the death of the Emperor Charles VI had placed his daughter, Maria Theresa, on the throne of Austria, with every prospect, a prospect that was amply fulfilled, that not only would her succession be disputed, but that there would be attempts from more quarters than one to filch away some of the vast possessions of Austria. The war, known as the War of the Austrian Succession, had indeed broken out within a few months. But before that, while the issues of war and peace yet hung in the balance, Frederick had struck. He had seized Breslau, the capital of the Austrian province of Silesia, with no declaration of war, and under pretexts which he himself later cynically admitted to have no foundation in fact. A campaign of a few months had seen him master of all Lower Silesia, and, two years later, when war had spread over half Europe, Maria Theresa had been forced to purchase his neutrality by ceding to him the province to which he had helped himself; he, in return, recognizing her claim to all the other Austrian possessions.

Yet, despite this triumph, no one knew better than the King of Prussia that he had aroused enmities which in the long run might, unless he played his hand skilfully, prove fatal to him, and to his country. During the following year his unease had been quickened by successes of Maria

Theresa in the field. He turned his gaze eastward.

There, to the east, beyond the kingdom of Poland, lay Russia, not yet fully drawn into the vortex of European politics; in the eyes of many in western Europe still a mysterious land, but one that, as observers of political affairs thought, would bear watching. Some years since, before the coup d'état of Elizabeth, Claudius Rondeau, sometime English envoy in St. Petersburg, had remarked that the court of Russia was beginning to have a good deal to say in the affairs of Europe. And Frederick, in his kingdom of Prussia, harboured no illusions. His correspondence makes it amply clear that from the beginning of his reign he had been aware of formidable potentialities in Russia; that therein lurked danger for himself, and for Prussia. At this moment he was more than ever on the watch, for the tide of opinion at the Russian court was, he learned from his agents, setting against him. In particular, Elizabeth's Vice-chancellor, Bestúzhev-Ryúmin, was his enemy. And the latter directed foreign policy. That policy was based on the Vice-chancellor's profound conviction that the growing might of Prussia under Frederick was a source of peril to Russia; and that therefore the proper course for the latter country to follow was support of Austria as against her aggressive neighbour. Frederick knew well enough what a military alliance between Russia and Austria against himself might imply. Such a union had to be prevented at all

8

costs; and Russia be at the very least kept neutral. That, for him, was of vital importance; and his consciousness of this had its repercussions at Stettin.

Within a very few days after the letter of the Empress had been received by the governor and his lady, there came to them another letter— from Frederick. In that letter the King of Prussia made it clear that he approved of a bride from one of his own provinces for the future ruler of Russia. What was looming as even more important in his mind, was the usefulness of a really trusty agent at the Russian court. That agent was to be Johanna, who, delighting in the rôle, had already shown that she was more than willing to play his game. So, between the Empress of Russia and the King of Prussia, was Sophie's course set.

There was no great delay in the making of the preparations for the journey, the cost of which was to be borne by the Empress, a fact not without importance to the family at Stettin, since German princes of their standing were not apt to be wealthy; and the family of Anhalt-Zerbst were no exception to the rule.

During those days of preparation the governor had a solemn interview with his daughter. It was an interview typical of such always and everywhere, the worthy, straight-laced, and, one suspects, dull princeling whose ambitions for himself probably soared no higher than the governorship to which he had attained, whatever was the case with his wife, taking farewell of the daughter before whom a great, but certainly difficult future was opening; giving her advice in a series of platitudes and homilies—in particular she should take no part in political affairs— bestowing on her for her reading a religious treatise.

Then, on 12 January, the carriages with father, mother, and daughter, and some five or six attendants, set forth—to Berlin. There they saw Frederick, who had every wish to see Johanna, of whom he expected much, and desired also to see the girl Sophie, and did so, in spite, if the latter's memoirs are to be credited, of a spirited attempt on the part of her mother to prevent an interview—Johanna always wanted attention focused on herself. Two days at Berlin; and the procession set out once more, making as if to return to Stettin, perhaps a ruse in accordance with the numerous instructions received as to secrecy, a secrecy not easy to obtain. It was not to Stettin that they went, but to Stargard, not so far away from the home town. There the governor left them. He went back to Stettin; his wife and daughter continued along the Baltic coast, by Danzig and Königsberg and Memel towards Riga, encountering, to their great thankfulness, no snow storm on the way, but meeting an icy wind, the piercing wind blowing from the Arctic, which impelled them to cover up their faces.

Riga was reached on 7 February, almost exactly four weeks after the little party had quitted Stargard; and with Riga, Russia. The Baltic port had become also a Russian port, when in 1721 Sweden had ceded Livonia to Peter the Great. The reception of the guests of the Empress on this their entrance into Russia was impressive, and amid other details, to mother and daughter were handed, as gifts from Elizabeth, cloaks of sable—the lovely Russian sable, esteemed throughout Europe—lined with gold brocade; and a rug of the same fur.

And so onwards. But now the manner of travel was changed. At Riga the carriages were left behind; and in their place were sleighs—the first, wrote Sophie, that she had ever seen—each sleigh drawn by ten horses.

The departure from Riga took place, according to the dating to which the travellers were accustomed, that of the reformed calendar now in general, though not universal, use in Europe, on 9 February. But even as the sleighs had replaced the carriages, so another, an older method of enumerating the days of the year marked the entrance into the Russian provinces; by the Muscovy calendar the year had receded eleven days, and it was now but 29 January.

Another four days, and St. Petersburg was reached, adopting the reckoning by which Russia ordered its days, on 3 February (14 February, N.S.).

The city which Peter had caused to be constructed on the swampy delta and the islands at the mouth of the Neva river, a city looking to the west, had now been the capital of Russia, save for an interval of a few years after Peter's death, since, some thirty-odd years back, the buildings had been sufficiently complete for its founder to order the removal of the government thither. It was a city of wood and stone, with, on its island, the fortress and cathedral of St. Peter and St. Paul. From the latter, holding the tomb of the man who had created the city, rose tall and slender the spire—a copy of that of the Bourse in Copenhagen—dominating the surroundings; but not yet, as it was later to be, glittering by reason of its plates of gilt and copper.

In general appearance, the capital of Russia, as Sophie first saw it, would not perhaps have seemed strange to the eyes of travellers from North Germany, since its buildings had been planned by Peter's deliberate choice after the German-Dutch style. But changes were already in making. The Winter Palace to which the sleighs drove was not Peter's wooden building. This one had been designed for Elizabeth by the young Italian architect Bartolommeo Rastrelli, and had been completed only some four years back. It stood on a site purchased by the Empress, between her father's palace and his Admiralty, and like them, it faced the Neva, now, in February, still and frozen.

In the palace, mother and daughter spent three days, while St. Petersburg outdid Riga in the splendour of the reception offered them; and when on the third day they set forth on the final stage of their journey, the four hundred and eighty-seven miles to Moscow, where the Empress awaited them, their procession took on a new magnificence; many more attendants, many more postillions for the horses which drew the sleighs, now thirty in number.

It had been impressed upon Johanna that they were expected to arrive in Moscow before 10 February (21 February, N.S.), in order that they might be present at the celebration of the sixteenth anniversary of the birthday of the youth who was formerly Charles Peter but who had lost his first name when he was baptized into the Orthodox Church as Peter Féodorovitch. To attain the goal in time haste had to be made indeed; and the pace of this last stage of the journey was very different from that made at the beginning. Every preparation in the way of posts along the road, booths with hot food and drinks, had been made. In the great sleighs, covered in and heated, really rooms on runners, used by such travellers, it was possible for the occupants to sleep as they went. Moreover, as far as the road was concerned, the winter was far the best time of year for travelling. Peter had planned a new highway, a broad causeway laid with trunks of trees, which should run from his new capital to the city which had been the capital. But only one hundred miles of this had been completed; and even this stretch was not, as travellers remarked, very good, while the remainder was very bad indeed. But, during the winter months, the frozen snow made a hard, smooth surface over which sleighs, particularly when drawn, as were these, by a great number of horses, could pass with ease and remarkable rapidity. So the procession went on through the short days and long nights by way of Tsarskoe Selo, the imperial spot where Peter had built for his wife Catherine a wooden palace, which had been given by her to her daughter Elizabeth; and by the ancient city of Novgorod; and by scattered villages, often consisting of a few wooden houses only; until, on the fourth day after they had left St. Petersburg, and nearly six weeks since they had quitted Stettin, on 6 February (17 February, N.S.), they arrived in the outskirts of Moscow. Now another six horses had been added to each sleigh; and now Sophie put on one of her new dresses, of which she had three in her luggage. This one was of rose-coloured moiré and silver. That evening, they made a formal entrance into Moscow.

Moscow, the capital for four centuries before Peter had built his city, stood for another Russia than St. Petersburg. It was a city which had perforce been rebuilt again and again after the conflagrations inevitable where buildings had been largely constructed and reconstructed of wood. But, throughout, Moscow had never lost its character. Few eighteenth-century travellers failed to comment on the intermingling of the east with the west; Asia jostling Europe; and no less the juxtaposition of wealth and poverty, with, as Sophie recorded in her memoirs, as much dirt and sordidness in the one as the other, only in the former case concealed by a veneer of magnificence. Everywhere churches and monasteries; and significant among the whole, the Kremlin, with its tower, the tower of Ivan the Great; its palace and its halls; its chapels, its courtyards; a little city in itself.

But it was not to the palace in the Kremlin that Sophie and her mother were driven, for, since the move to St. Petersburg, the Kremlin was no longer the royal residence, although still used for official occasions. The procession drove right across the city to the palace, in which the Empress was in residence; one of the two palaces, the Annenhof and the Golivin, which stood side by side on the far bank of the little river called the Yauza, a tributary of the Moskva, which ran beneath the walls of the Kremlin, and from which the city took its name. Then followed the reception by the Empress.

It was the age of elegant splendour in Europe, of clothes as of all else, with the court at Versailles setting the note. To France the Empress looked for her fashions; but she added to them, like the

15

court of which she was the head, something that was Russian, something that reflected the colour, the gorgeousness of the east. Handsome, with robust good looks which she had inherited from her sturdy, peasant mother, voluptuous, sensual, Elizabeth is represented as always a splendid show; making full use of the possibilities offered to any woman whose expenditure knows no limitations. Her biographers rarely fail to mention that she had fifteen thousand dresses in her wardrobe when she died; with the addenda that she seldom, if ever, paid her bills, either those for her costumes, or those of her French milliner. This evening her dress was of silver taffeta, that shimmering, metallic material so characteristic of the day. In her hair were diamonds and a long black plume. She moved, in her huge hooped skirt, as Sophie noted, with that dignity, grace, and even lightness, which belong to a stout woman. A traveller in Russia, Dr. John Cook, had remarked on that lightness of movement years before. On such an occasion as this, when the easy good nature which was one of her attributes could have full play, the Empress was perhaps at her best. But behind that easy good nature was the determination which had brought her to the throne, and kept her there.

After the reception by the Empress, followed another meeting. Strictly speaking, the introduction of the young man who was to be ruler of Russia to his future bride was a formal introduction only, for the two had already met as children in the course of one of the many tours on which Johanna had taken her daughter. On that occasion, it was said, the girl of ten years old had not been favourably impressed by the boy of eleven years. She had found his appearance—he was pale and delicate-looking—unprepossessing, and even more unprepossessing his greedy behaviour at meals, in the matter of drink as well as of food. There was much to justify those who, knowing Sophie at her father's court, had perceived in her, at a very early age, a power of detached criticism. The fifteen-year-old girl would have been something less than human had she not, at this significant moment, looked at the sixteen-year-old youth, whom she knew was to be her betrothed, with attention. In her case, it was likely to be with critical attention. She may well have found him no more attractive than he had appeared earlier. He was still sickly-looking, and diplomatists, who were not concerned to make the worst of the unfortunate young man, had long noted the loutish bearing which was the outward expression of the dull, narrow mind. They had seen something more. During his three years at the Russian court, he had not adapted himself as it had been hoped he would do. Duke of Holstein-Gottorp in succession to his father, he had been made a Grand-duke of Russia. The latter title took precedence of the first. All possible Russian influence had been brought to bear upon the holder. He remained, in his tastes, his ideas, his whole outlook, entirely German.

To the strength of the German strain, accompanied as it was by a fanatical admiration for Prussia, was attributed what appeared to be the one passion of the young man's life, his fondness for drilling soldiers, toy soldiers at first, then live men. One gentle trait he did possess. He played the fiddle. It was unfortunate that this accomplishment was precisely the one which would not appeal to his bride, who was always said to have been, if not tone deaf, at least definitely unmusical.

But whatever the young couple may have thought of one another, their course was set. Royalties were not usually given a choice in the matter of marriage anywhere, and certainly not at this court.

Not that it was to be an immediate marriage. There was one essential preliminary. The bride-to-be must be received into the communion of the Greek or Orthodox Church. Perhaps it was with this in mind that the governor of Stettin had bestowed upon his daughter, for her reading, that religious treatise. It was said that he disliked the idea of the change of faith, and that Johanna did not inform him of the ceremony until it had taken place. He must, however, have known that it was inevitable.

Four months of instruction preceded the reception. They were months which held something more of import. During them Sophie had a bad attack of pleurisy, an illness which for a short time caused much alarm. It was an illness punctuated by quarrels over the sick-bed between the Empress Elizabeth and the Princess Johanna of Anhalt-Zerbst. Those ladies, after a few months of each other's acquaintance, were by no means on the best of terms with one another. At all times but especially now in the sick-chamber Johanna desired, not unnaturally, to exercise the maternal influence which she felt to be her right over her daughter; and in this had permitted herself to come into opposition to the Empress, who had no doubt whose influence should be paramount.

Another and deeper cause of friction existed. Johanna had been trying her hand at the work which Frederick had designed for her; and Elizabeth and her advisers, especially her Vice-chancellor, against whom the intrigue was more particularly directed, were beginning to suspect as much.

By the end of April the invalid was well on the way to recovery. In June she was pronounced to be sufficiently instructed to be received into the Orthodox Church, henceforth to be her church. Her confession of faith was made, and her reception took place on 28 June in the palace chapel. During the rites she was baptized afresh, as had been her husband-to-be. She took the names of Catherine Alexandrovna.

The girl who henceforth must be called
Catherine subsequently compared what she had
done with the reception of Henry IV of France
into the Roman communion; and, doubtless, in
the proceeding, there was something, even much,
of the attitude of mind, that if the throne of France
was worth a Mass, then that of Russia was worth
the transference from the Lutheran to the
Orthodox Church. Not that she had any real
choice in the matter. But there is no reason to
suppose that the acceptance of another doctrine,
of other rites and ceremonies, to those in which
she had been brought up in Stettin, was made
unwillingly. In later years, the mature woman,
Catherine the Empress, was to show herself
completely at one with that school of eighteenth-
century philosophers, many among whom became
her friends, whose attitude to varying forms of
religion was that of detached and academic
tolerance. In that spirit the girl of fifteen may
well have accepted the change of church. But it
is also possible to see, in the great ceremony of
the reception, led up to by her studies with her
instructor, an early landmark in her progress
towards identification of herself with Russia.

The religious service completed, that evening
the court moved into the palace of the Kremlin.
The following day, in the Chapel of the
Assumption, the most magnificent and most
venerated of the chapels of the Kremlin, the
coronation place of the Tsars, with the jewelled

ikon of the Holy Virgin of Vladimir conspicuous among all the other jewelled ikons and shrines of gold and silver, Catherine and Peter were solemnly betrothed. At the same time Catherine was given the rank of a Grand-duchess of Russia.

The double ceremony called forth a letter of congratulation from the King of Prussia. To the letter Catherine sent a very proper reply, and included a sentence of acknowledgment of the part Frederick had played in the matter.

Shortly after the conclusion of the two great functions, the Grand-duke Peter and his betrothed were commanded by the Empress to take a journey with her. In the course of that journey they came to yet another Russia, neither that of St. Petersburg, nor of Moscow, but the Russia of which the capital was Kiev, the mother city of all the Russian cities. Here, until a series of Mongol invasions had culminated in the middle of the thirteenth century with the terrible sacking of the great city, had been the seat of the rulers of Russia; and here, too, had been the centre of a civilization as cultured, as learned, as artistic, as any in Europe. After the Mongols had been driven out, first Lithuania, and then Poland had claimed Kiev. In 1667, more than three hundred years since the Mongolian hordes had made it their own, it had become once more a Russian city.

Standing on the west bank of the river Dnieper, Catherine noted, what many others were to note after her, how fine was the view of the city from the river bank. Met by a concourse of clergy, the royal party crossed the river to proceed on foot in procession, headed by an acolyte bearing aloft a cross, to the great monastery or Lavra set with the cathedral high on a hill above the city. Nothing, wrote Catherine later, had ever impressed her like that cathedral with its splendours of gold and silver and jewels; although she observed with distaste certain practices which appeared to her to be merely superstitious. Neither she nor the Grand-duke was permitted to visit the catacombs which, in their degree, were as famous as the cathedral itself. The air in the catacombs was said to be dangerously bad and, in view of comments by other travellers, such may well have been the case.

The Grand-duke did not, however, escape illness. It was in the course of this journey, perhaps during the stay at Kiev, that the always unfortunate young man was seized by smallpox, the disease that was endemic over the greater part of Europe, not excluding the British Isles. Nor was he more fortunate than others in the marks which the complaint left upon its victims. It was noted that the pitting of the skin had rendered an always unpleasing and unwholesome countenance yet more unattractive; and some writers see, in the aftermath of the infection, a contributory cause to the beginning of Catherine's distaste for her bridegroom.

Even if distaste did not already exist, adjustments had inevitably and constantly to be made in her relations with the Grand-duke, and not only with him. She herself laid stress on the difficulties that she, a girl not yet sixteen years of age, experienced in her endeavour to please at one and the same time the Empress and her mother. Elizabeth might be good-natured. She was also an autocrat. As for Johanna, the exceeding unwisdom of her behaviour, based on her intrigues, was aggravated by her lack of even ordinary tact in her intercourse with Elizabeth. The months before her marriage cannot have been easy for Catherine.

The marriage was celebrated, after two postponements, in the following year, on 25 August, 1745. It took place, not in Moscow, but in St. Petersburg; in the church of Our Lady of Kazan, the wooden-roofed church which stood in the great street laid out by Peter the Great's architects, the Nevsky Prospect, on the site where the cathedral of the same name was afterwards to stand. It had been built by the Empress Anne, to house, as the dedication implied, the miraculous ikon of the Virgin, removed from Kazan when in 1579 that city, standing on the Volga, was freed from Mongol rule, first to Moscow, and then to St. Petersburg. Now the edifice was recognized as that closely associated with the imperial court, particularly for services of thanksgiving.

In that church, wearing a robe of cloth of silver,

and on her head the high jewelled Russian crown or tiara, Catherine was married to Peter. The festivities which followed, and which lasted for ten days, were modelled on those of other weddings which had taken place, neither in St. Petersburg nor yet in Moscow, but in Dresden and at Versailles, the description of which Elizabeth had been at pains to secure. And, noted Johanna in the memoirs which she, too, in common with so many others, men and women of the day, wrote for herself, they were as magnificent as anything ever seen in all Europe.

This was the last that Johanna was ever to see of Russia, or of her daughter, or of the life in which she had so rejoiced. It was now intimated to her beyond any possibility of misunderstanding that she was required to return to Stettin; and return she did, not without substantial mementoes of Russia, for, to the last, as far as material things went, Elizabeth was generous enough. That was part of her character. Whisperers went further and said that Johanna had taken more than a fair advantage of that generosity, even to the cases of china which accompanied her from Russia. But in diplomacy Johanna had played her game and lost, as the King of Prussia was to learn.

Chapter Two

The Grand-duchess

THE English minister at the court of Russia had remarked of the Princess of Anhalt-Zerbst that she was a lady who was not easily rebutted. Nevertheless, no success had attended her machinations on behalf of Frederick: she herself must have been aware that this was so for at least a year before her daughter's marriage to the heir of the throne and her own departure from Russia.

Matters had come to a head during Catherine's illness in the spring and early summer of the previous year. The quarrels over her sick-bed had had a deeper significance than mere rivalry between the Empress Elizabeth and the Princess Johanna as to who had the better right to control the invalid and her way of life, for the political intrigues of Johanna, long suspected and even partially known, were at that moment being proved up to the hilt. The man who was chiefly instrumental in uncovering those intrigues and making them clear to the Empress, was the man against whom they had been chiefly directed.

In that year of 1744 Bestúzhev-Ryúmin, usually known by the first part of his name, was fifty-one years of age, and had served a long apprenticeship in diplomacy, beginning under Peter the Great, chiefly in posts outside Russia. Elizabeth, on her succession, had brought him back to work at home and made him Vice-chancellor. He it was who had drawn up her first ukase.

It was said of Bestúzhev that he was far more feared than loved. Nor was his character, according to most evidence, a lovable one. For he was said to be difficult and moody; and withal a master of intrigue and a lover of power. If, as the historian Herzen later remarked, he could show himself a good friend, he could also be a very bad enemy.

That he himself should have enemies both at home and abroad was inevitable. France, already more than a little suspicious of the growing power of Russia, which might easily threaten the balance of power in northern and eastern Europe, was well aware of the importance of Bestúzhev, who stood, as they knew, for a strong Russia. The French ambassador, the Marquis de la Chétardie, had some years since been instructed to keep a very close watch on what was going on. Frederick of Prussia for his part, his kingdom lying so much further eastward, had no doubt at all what ought to be done. Bestúzhev stood for Austria and against Prussia. Therefore he must be dealt with. The instructions to Johanna had been a more or less direct command to get rid of Bestúzhev, or at least to nullify his influence with Elizabeth.

This was a piece of work after Johanna's own heart, implying the pulling of strings and, as she hoped, the secret exercise of power in which her heart delighted. There was little difficulty in finding other persons who were more than willing to play the game with her since it was their game also. De la Chétardie, on behalf of his country, and from his own observations, was in cordial agreement with Frederick that the dismissal of Bestúzhev must be contrived. He and the French agents accepted Johanna's overtures with zeal. So, although to a lesser degree, did those among the ministers and in Elizabeth's household who were the Vice-chancellor's personal enemies. Among the last were prominent two brothers, Alexander and Peter Shuvalov. To them, gentlemen of her household, the Empress owed a debt of gratitude for support given when she had seized the throne. Yet, although they were duly rewarded by wealth and position, it was Bestúzhev, whom Elizabeth is always said to have disliked personally, as so many others disliked him, who had been given high office.

The intrigues, with the secret instructions coming from Frederick and from France, had been cleverly worked but not quite cleverly enough. The Vice-chancellor had his own sources of information and was no stranger to the game of intrigue. In June 1744, he had been able to lay before the Empress convincing evidence of what had been going on. The evidence included the revelation of the secret correspondence of the French ambassador with avowed enemies of Russia, in particular with Sweden; and the no less reprehensible correspondence of Johanna with Frederick and others.

Before the month was out de la Chétardie had been escorted to the Russian frontier. Johanna, closely watched, had been allowed to remain until the marriage of the following year. Bestúzhev was promoted from the office of Vice-chancellor to that of Chancellor and the promotion was marked by an extensive gift of lands and a palace; the customary recognition for services done for the crown. For him it was at once a personal triumph and a wholehearted endorsement of the anti-Prussian policy.

But neither the Empress nor her Chancellor, however closely they might watch Prussia, however dangerous they might esteem Frederick's military successes to be, were as yet prepared to plunge Russia into war. In 1748 the War of the Austrian Succession came to an end without the direct participation of Russia. Nevertheless, a Russian corps had, during the last year of the war, crossed the Vistula and, entering Germany, made its way to the Rhine. The men did no fighting; but there were not lacking observers in Europe who saw the occurrence as a portent.

For Prussia and its king the Treaty of Aix-la-Chapelle, closing the war, was a triumph. Frederick emerged not only with his seizure of

Silesia ratified, but with a reputation of which Europe had perforce to take note. For a few years the continent knew an uneasy peace.

In Russia, the young Grand-duke and duchess lived amid surroundings which, externally at least, were always grand and often magnificent. Everywhere rebuilding was in process; not confined to the capital, for work was being done in Moscow, as in Kiev. Nevertheless, it was St. Petersburg in particular which was now to be transformed—as the Winter Palace had already been transformed—by the genius of Bartolommeo Rastrelli and his fellow architects, from the German-Dutch city of its founder into one of Franco-Italian rococo; elegant, like the Empress; extravagant, like the Empress; and always, despite the foreign origin, Russian.

In Moscow a residence was provided for the young couple by the addition of a wing to the Golivin Palace on the banks of the Yauza. In St. Petersburg they were given apartments in the Winter and Summer Palaces. There were other palaces, outside the city. Among them, to the south of the capital, was Tsarskoe Selo; and on the Gulf of Finland were Peterhof and Oranienbaum. The Grand-duke and his duchess had their rooms in Tsarskoe Selo and in the palace of Peterhof; both buildings in the process of being worked on by Rastrelli. Oranienbaum was given over to them for their particular use.

Situated some twenty-five miles along the coast

from St. Petersburg and six from Peterhof, the palace of Oranienbaum had been erected by a lieutenant of Peter the Great, one of the first of the princely residences to be built in the vicinity of the capital, taking its name, as did others also, from the village by which it stood. Then disgrace had overtaken the owner and his palace had become an imperial palace. For the Grand-duke and his duchess, the building having become a good deal the worse for wear, alterations were effected by Rastrelli's compatriot, Antonio Rinaldi, who, leaving much of the original structure intact, added pavilions and a Chinese house, those devices beloved of the eighteenth-century architect. Outside, the balustraded garden terraces of the days of Peter the Great led down to the waters of the gulf across which could be seen the fortress of Cronstadt.

In this palace of Oranienbaum and in the other palaces, where were found the splendour of the east and the elegance of the west, but where magnificence concealed, as Catherine had long ago observed when she first saw Moscow, something very like squalor, comfort mingling with discomfort, everyday life as prescribed for the young couple was, as far as authority could make it, hemmed around. There was a code of rules to be followed under rigid and close surveillance.

The rules were laid down and the surveillance was provided for in two sets of instructions. They had been drawn up by the Chancellor with the approval of the Empress.

In any event, for it was nothing more than in accordance with court custom, regulations would have been set forth for the guidance of the young couple, the behaviour expected of them, what their manner of life should in general be. That the Grand-duke was heir to the throne necessarily implied for him and for his wife the observance of such conventions and restrictions. More than this, no official of experience was likely to lose sight of the danger, a latent danger wherever there were two courts, that the lesser court might become not only a focal point for court camarillas, but a centre of political intrigue, both domestic and foreign. It was a risk that no authority could afford to take and Bestúzhev knew it. That the systems prescribed for the observance of the Grand-duke and duchess went considerably beyond the usual code was in great part due to his belief that in this case the danger was peculiarly acute.

He had justification for his belief. The Grand-duke Peter had become the admiring and wholly uncritical disciple of the King of Prussia. This hero worship, for it was nothing more and nothing less, of Peter for Frederick must be assigned in the first instance to the strong racial feeling in which the German inheritance from his father totally eclipsed the Russian inheritance from his mother. But with this, and reinforcing it, went the ever-growing passion for militarism, or at all events, for playing at militarism, long since observed in the boy and now, in the young man, amounting to a mania. Lastly, there must be taken into account what was becoming in Peter yet more apparent as time went on; the neurotic symptoms of a young man placed in a high position which he was unfitted to fill, surrounded by difficulties with which he was unfitted to cope. So he found an outlet in his idolatry of Frederick, a travesty not without pathos of the dictum that to believe in the heroic makes a hero.

It was small wonder that Bestúzhev, whose opinions on the Prussian danger had changed no whit, should view the predilection of the Grand-duke for the Prussian King with distrust and apprehension. Nor was the Chancellor satisfied that trouble would not come from the Grand-duchess. He could forget neither Catherine's origins—German birth on both sides—nor yet the part played by her mother, that lively, intriguing and highly dangerous lady. So the preamble to the charge issued for the guidance of the governor and governess of the lesser court ordered that any interest displayed by the Grand-duchess in political affairs was to be checked at once. From the Chancellor's point of view, this was an entirely logical proceeding. It was also one that might contain the seeds of a good deal of trouble. A further definite order was that Catherine's correspondence with her mother should be strictly supervised.

Catherine's early life had been spent under all the rigour of a small German court. She was now governed, interfered with, watched over, as never before. That the scheme which now regulated her life, and that of her husband, had been drawn up by Bestúzhev she was well aware; and she was no more inclined at this moment to look upon him with favour than he so to look upon her. To the Chancellor the young woman was a possible source of danger; and, she later wrote with considerable vehemence, he took pleasure in any humiliation it was possible to put upon her.

Bestúzhev was not the only one who on occasion took pleasure in humiliating Catherine. It was observed that the Empress was often rude to the young Grand-duchess in public and that any friendliness or kindness the older woman had once shown the wife of her heir almost entirely ceased. Jealousy had something to say in the matter; resentment at the strength of character which Elizabeth was far too shrewd not to divine; the strength of character which lay beneath Catherine's submissiveness; and disappointment. Disappointment as it was borne in upon the Empress what manner of man her nephew, of whom she had hoped so much, really was. Disappointment at Catherine's failure, after several years of marriage, to produce an heir.

Hence petty and intensely irritating persecutions of both Grand-duke and Grand-duchess; and above all, the deliberate isolating of the younger court from all affairs of importance, though never any relaxation of the watch kept on every detail of the life lived therein day by day.

Here the Grand-duke and Grand-duchess suffered alike; and here, and only here, was there any sympathy between them. It was not sufficient to bring together a couple to whom a few years of marriage had revealed their complete incompatibility one with the other.

Despite the Empress, despite the Chancellor, the vital factor for Catherine during those years when she was growing into maturity—she was nineteen when the Peace of Aix-la-Chapelle was signed in 1748—must have been the character of her husband, even making allowance for the conventional, almost artificial view of marriage that obtained in the eighteenth century, at any rate in court and aristocratic circles.

In her later analysis of the situation, Catherine accentuated the gulf between Peter's tastes and her own, the complete lack of any intellectual sympathy between them. She would, she wrote, have liked to read with him, but he cared only for tales of bandits and those had no interest for her. Nor could she, unfortunately, abide Peter's fiddle, on which she declared he merely made ear-splitting sounds. But the fact that Catherine, a clever girl, rapidly growing into a very able woman, was married to a man of, at the best, limited intelligence, need not have made the marriage a failure, certainly did not account for all that was to come after. She had genuinely wished to love Peter, continued Catherine, it was his debauched habits which revolted her.

The unfortunate Grand-duke may or may not have been quite so debauched as was later represented. Allowance must be made for the emphasis later placed on his unpleasing qualities by his widow, defending herself, and by those who were concerned to defend her. That he had mistresses meant, in that age and in those circles, little or nothing. Nor is it probable his wife would have raised any serious objections to such diversions, even though she felt herself justified in resenting her husband's remark, in the third week of their marriage, that he greatly preferred 'Fräulein Carr'—a lady of the household, of Scottish origin—to her. But such tales—and there were many of them—as those of horrible cruelty to his pet dogs, and a curious story of a rat he sentenced to die, military fashion, by his own sword, have, it is more than likely, some foundation in fact, as also those of his violence when drunk. There is corroboration to some extent from even those who wished him well.

Life as Grand-duchess was not easy for Catherine. Always there must have been the sense of being cribbed, cabined and confined: spied upon, in her bedroom, in the great salons of whatever palace in which the lesser court was living, as she walked along the terraced gardens of Oranienbaum. Always there was the hard fact

35

of the marriage tie between her and a husband with whom she was ever less and less in sympathy, and, further, for whose personal habits she was ever feeling more and yet more distaste.

Certain alleviations offered themselves. She and the Empress had at least one taste in common. Both were passionately fond of dancing; and both were expert in that art. Catherine's other devotion was to riding. This accomplishment she is said to have acquired only after her arrival in Russia. Having acquired it, she indulged in it with fervour, insisting on riding astride, to the fury of the Empress, who forbade this form of equitation. The prohibition was circumvented by Catherine finding, or having found for her, a saddle which could be used for any style of riding.

Catherine, in short, even in such a small matter, was, in the circumstances in which she found herself, taking her life into her own hands.

And not in such a small matter only. Partly, perhaps, unconsciously, partly consciously, she was wresting advantage from her circumstances in giving herself what has been called her second education. She was reading voraciously.

It was quite in character that this reading should, it is said, have included every Russian book on which she could lay her hands. From the first she had set herself to learn the Russian language as thoroughly as she might. That was part of the process of which Bestúzhev, for one, had, at any rate at first, entirely failed to grasp the significance.

There were Russian books at hand. The first printing press in Russia had been set up in 1564, by Ivan the Terrible. Throughout the next century learning had been stimulated by the arrival in Moscow of scholars from Kiev, whose tradition of learning had been buried under the Mongol invasions but had not been killed and was now reviving. Peter the Great had founded the first Russian newspaper and he had ordained a simplification of the Russian script. Here, however, as everywhere, Peter also looked west, and he had ordered many translations of foreign books. After his death foreign influence, the influence pre-eminently of Germany and of France, became supreme in the Russian world of books. That influence remained supreme for many years to come, even though when Catherine was thus continuing her education, some stirring of the soil which held the seeds of the future flowers of Russian literature was already apparent. Michael Lomonosov, the son of a peasant of Archangel, a poet and a scholar, was breaking new ground in his writings in Russian. The foundation of the first Russian university, that of Moscow, was at hand.

Nevertheless, by far the greater part of what Catherine read in Russian must have been modelled on foreign authors and have been in consequence only too often stilted and pedantic in style. In the long run it was other literature, the literature of France, the expression of French

37

thought, in which her mind became soaked.

Beginning with such volumes as the *Letters of Madame de Sévigné*, the works of Brantôme, of Rabelais and of Montaigne, of Molière and of Corneille, she turned presently to Tacitus, of whose *Annals* she wrote that the reading of them had worked a peculiar revolution in her mind. But two other writers exercised yet stronger influence. She had commenced to read Voltaire as early as 1744; and in that same year she is also said to have been recommended, by one of her well-wishers at court, to read the two notable books which had given Montesquieu his place in the literary world. Neither *On the Causes of the Grandeur and Decline of the Romans*, nor the earlier *Persian Letters*, had, however, appealed to her. But in 1748 appeared the *Spirit of the Laws*; and upon this she is quoted as having fallen in ecstasy. That ecstasy was a source of later inspiration.

Catherine herself later stressed the consolation that she, in her gilded cage, had found in her studies. But neither books, nor much less riding and dancing, and other courtly amusements, completely filled her life. She had another side to her nature and that side demanded satisfaction.

The Grand-duchess was perhaps twenty-two or twenty-three years of age when she had her first liaison—with the court chamberlain, Sergei Saltikov. He was a young man of whom she wrote, that he was as beautiful as the day, so that no one high or low had ever been his like. The good looks were generally conceded but according to his critics the young man had not otherwise much to recommend him. The French Ambassador went so far as to say that he was ignorant, tasteless, and in short, without any merit whatsoever. Howsoever this may have been, the connection with Saltikov shows itself in some respects as more pleasing than those with others which came after: in so far as it may be seen as the not unnatural outcome of the situation in which Catherine found herself in relation to her husband —a young woman, desiring love, desiring the fulfilment of her natural instincts, tied in a marriage without affection to a man whose physical and mental characteristics were, at the best, unpleasing and, in the eyes of many, repulsive.

But this first affair can also be taken as a pointer to the other and later adventures in love. Catherine was more and more to show herself as frankly sensual. In that sensuality, she also showed herself capable of something like real affection. But withal, although the heart keeps its own secrets, everything in the life of the Grand-duchess, as of the Empress that was to be, implies that passion was not at any time her master. The quality of her mind was ever reinforced by the cool, calculating ambition that, however concealed at the moment, penetrating observers had already perceived in the adolescent girl. It was a Russian historian who later emphasized the dictum of Ernest Renan: that history which sought to be true should not pay excessive attention to the personal manners and customs of rulers, when these had not greatly influenced the course of events. This most sensible saying, wrote Brian-Chianinov, should be kept in mind when considering Catherine and her lovers. Certainly her relations with each and every one of those lovers, whatever affection and kindliness she might for the time being feel towards them, was for Catherine a passing phase. It is doubtful, did the phase endure over months or years, whether she ever lost control of herself or of the situation. And, while some of the lovers in particular played their parts in the pattern of the life and work of the Empress, Renan's aphorism may be accepted as true of the main scheme of that life and work.

Sergei Saltikov soon disappeared. He was sent to Stockholm in the diplomatic service and so got rid of within a very short space of time.

But it was while he was still in attendance on Catherine that an event, one for which the Empress Elizabeth had been eagerly awaiting, an event of significance for the present as for the future, had taken place. In 1754 a living child, and that child a son, was at last born to Catherine.

Given the circumstances, quite well known at any rate in the circles of the two courts, it was inevitable that there should have been at the time, and should continue to be later, speculation as to whether the Grand-duke or the handsome Saltikov was the child's father. On the whole the paternity of the former was, and has been, generally, though not universally, accepted. As the boy grew older he was said to show a marked physical resemblance to the Grand-duke; certain traits in his character might well be seen as an inheritance from the same source. The fact that Catherine never cared for her son, even to displaying at times active dislike of him, was not infrequently cited as further proof that he was her child by her husband. But it must be admitted that she was not allowed the opportunity to know or to grow fond of her child during the early years of his life. Elizabeth, delighted with the long-wished-for birth of an heir, an event which she hoped would ensure continuance of the line, had the infant taken away from his mother almost immediately after his birth, in order that he might be brought up under her own particular care. This arbitrary separation of mother and child may well, in part at least, explain the later relations between the two. In the immediate present, the action of the Empress had the result of widening the gulf between Catherine and her husband. It also widened the breach, already so apparent to the more acute observers of both courts, between Catherine and the Empress; between the lesser court and the greater.

Once more Catherine, thrown back upon herself with even more emphasis than before, can be seen at her books. Her mind, her ever-active, assimilative mind, now found new material on which to feed. In 1750 Denis Diderot had produced his scheme to collect into an encyclopædia all active writers, all new ideas, and all new knowledge: and 1751 had seen the publication of the first volume. This was precisely the kind of work to appeal to Catherine. During the early years of the seventeen-fifties she was turning to Diderot, D'Alembert, and the whole school of the encyclopædists. And always she was reading Voltaire— Voltaire, who during those years was visiting Frederick in Berlin, quarrelling with him, and finally, after sojourns in various German cities, arriving at Geneva; having begun the collection of the writings contributed and to be contributed to the encyclopædia, to appear as his *Dictionary of Philosophy*. It was this work that now particularly attracted Catherine's attention.

Contact with the ideas expressed by the philosophers from whose influence the age of reason took its name, marked a stage in Catherine's intellectual development. The course of events at the Russian court and elsewhere drew her, at the same time, from contemplative to other, more active, interests. In the midst of her reading, she was beginning to play her part in the game of politics.

As far back as 1749 the Empress Elizabeth had had a serious illness, from which she had not at one moment been expected to recover. She did recover, but those around her saw her henceforth as an ageing woman, although in years only in middle life. The full-blown peasant stock was, perhaps, prone to premature exhaustion; and, in any case, Elizabeth, in her mode of life, had taken many liberties with the robust health she had inherited from her Lithuanian mother. As the vigour, if not the life, of any man or woman in a prominent position can be seen to be on the wane, there arises inevitably speculation and, too often, intrigue as well. The Russian court was no exception to the rule; and everything in the past history of the Russian crown emphasized the apprehensions, the hopes, the secret schemes, excited and induced by a possible demise of that crown. The lesser court, Catherine with her ambition, her cool foresight, Peter with his own ideas, were alive to changes which seemed to be impending: which, even if delayed, must come. In official circles, Bestúzhev and his enemies the Shuvalovs, who had always kept their position near the Empress, watched her and watched each other. Nor did they forget the heir to the throne and his wife.

There is evidence that at least as early as 1754, the year of the birth of Catherine's son, Bestúzhev, although his position at court, despite his enemies, was still stable, and his influence with the Empress undiminished, had begun to make new dispositions in that he was casting a meditative eye on the younger court, and on one person in that court

43

in particular. That he was now convinced of the ineptitude of Peter and, in contrast, of the ability and strength of character of Catherine is clear. He made an approach to Catherine, and from Catherine came response. In August, 1754, she wrote to her mother, with whom she always kept up a correspondence, that she was delighted to know that the latter approved this close but very secret affiliation between herself and the Chancellor. Whether the two liked each other any better than they had ever done, what was the private view each of the other, mattered little. What was of vital importance was the recognition by each of the useful part the other might play. From this time onwards, Catherine was drawn into that vortex of politics against which her father, in taking leave of her, had so urgently warned her. That hoary warning of father to daughter had been fundamentally sound. It was, as one of Catherine's biographers, Dr. Alexander Brückner, has pointed out, quite unthinkable that Catherine would, in the long run, heed it. And now, having embarked on her new course, all she had learnt in the previous years from her reading, from the bitter draughts she had been forced to swallow by the Empress, no less than by Bestúzhev himself, from her observation of the life around her, served her well. That she and the Chancellor were contemplating what might befall on the death of the Empress is clear. It may be that

Bestúzhev was already thinking in terms of the putting aside of the Grand-duke and the substitution on the throne of the young son with a regency for Catherine.

But politics at home were inextricably mixed up with, and their course to a great extent directed by, affairs in Europe. As the period of feverish repose which followed the peace of 1748 drew to a close, it became evident that the renewal of war in Europe, with Prussia and Austria as principal antagonists, was merely a question of time. At St. Petersburg, the Chancellor had no doubt as to the policy that should, under the circumstances, be pursued by Russia. As he had ever been so he was still convinced, that Frederick of Prussia was a menace to Europe in general and Russia in particular. Therefore, as he saw it, there must be renewed alliance with, and support of, Austria. But he had also been working for another alliance. In the coming struggle, France would, he believed, maintain her traditional enmity towards Austria. And he disliked and distrusted France almost as much as he disliked and distrusted Prussia, not only on political, but on personal grounds. It was the French Ambassador and French agents who had played their part with the Princess of Anhalt-Zerbst in her endeavour, as commissioned by Frederick, to secure his own downfall. It was, however, evident to him, as to all, that France and England were once again about to grapple one with the other outside Europe. The logical course to pursue was, considered the Chancellor, to work for an Anglo-Russian alliance. In the arrival in St. Petersburg, in 1755, of a new English minister, he saw his chance.

The new arrival was Sir Charles Hanbury-Williams, a man of parts, a satirical poet as well as a diplomatist, who had served at Dresden and at Berlin. Since his instructions were to secure an understanding with Russia as a bulwark against a possible attack by Frederick upon the electorate of Hanover, the path of the negotiations entered upon almost immediately on his arrival seemed smooth enough. And so, for the time being, it proved. On 19 September, 1755, a convention was signed between the two countries. Russia was to keep 50,000 men on the Livonian frontier ready, if and when necessary, to march into Prussian territory; and was also to deploy a number of galleys along the coast. In return England promised an annual subsidy of £100,000 which would be quintupled should the troops and galleys be used in war.

In England the convention was in accordance with the foreign policy of the Duke of Newcastle, who had taken office the previous year. It was a policy founded on a system of alliances in return for subsidies. But the negotiations had also been carried through, as William Pitt and his followers saw, and disapproved what they saw, in deference to the determination of George II to secure, at all costs, the safety of Hanover, so dear to his heart.

Pitt, however, had been dismissed from his office of paymaster-general; and the King, Newcastle and Sir Charles Hanbury-Williams on the one side and Bestúzhev on the other had accomplished their aim. To the Chancellor, all seemed to be going well.

Frederick, never forgetting the menace from his eastern neighbour, was thoroughly startled by the drawing together of that neighbour and England, and thoroughly alarmed by the terms of an agreement between them which would in the event of war bring an incursion of Russian troops into Prussia. He knew the importance of Hanover in the eyes of George II. An approach on that subject had, indeed, already been made to him. He now made an approach in his turn. In January, 1756, not four months after what he had seen as a triumph, the Russian Chancellor was thunderstruck to learn that another convention had been signed; this time between Great Britain and Prussia. Known as the convention of Westminster, it provided that Prussia and Hanover should respect each other's neutrality; and that neither of the two should permit the entry of a foreign army on to German soil.

Frederick was well pleased. Across the water, Newcastle had apparently persuaded himself that this convention was not incompatible with that signed a few months earlier with Russia. At the same time Pitt and his followers accepted the new agreement. Pitt had no more liking than before

47

for any transaction carried through in the interests of Hanover. But the ominous implications of the ever-growing power of France out-weighed other considerations. That country was already challenging England on the high seas and in the possessions beyond the seas. Did she, as seemed might well be the case, over-run Europe, the invasion of England, for which she was known to be preparing, became not a probability but a certainty; and England was, at the moment, as Pitt well knew, almost defenceless. In such circumstances, an arrangement with Frederick was highly desirable.

The news of the earlier convention between England and Russia had already aroused the anger of France. At that of the convention of Westminster the anger became fury. An emissary was promptly sent off to Berlin to ask for an explanation. Frederick's endeavours to smooth the matter over by explaining that his agreement with England by no means implied hostility on his part towards France were completely unsuccessful. France turned her back on Prussia and looked towards her ancient enemy, Austria. The time was propitious. Austria was still smarting under the rape of Silesia, and the Austrian Chancellor, Kaunitz, favoured an approach to France. He now had little difficulty in persuading his Empress that the obliteration of the ancient enmity between Austria and France was well worth while if it meant the destruction of Frederick and the recovery of the stolen province.

In May, 1756, the treaty of Versailles, bringing
Austria and France together, put the coping stone
on the change in the diplomatic situation in
central and western Europe. Three months later,
on 27 August, Frederick, seeing himself threatened
by this formidable coalition, repeated his opening
move of the last struggle; and marched into
Saxony without the formality of a declaration of
war. The conflict that was to be known as The
Seven Years War had begun. It remained for
Russia to decide on her course of action.

To the unfortunate Bestúzhev, as in a lesser
degree to Sir Charles Hanbury-Williams, the
announcement of the signing of the convention
of Westminster had been a shattering blow. The
earlier treaty on which the two had spent so much
pains, and which the Chancellor had believed to
be essential as part of Russia's foreign policy, was
now, as both men saw, whatever Newcastle in
England might say, no more than waste paper.
Likewise Bestúzhev knew, beyond any possibility
of doubt, how greatly the whole affair had weakened his own standing with Elizabeth, even though
he retained his office and to outward appearances
the position was as before.

Awareness of the growing strength of his
enemies at court, as well as the continued conviction that the Empress would not live into old age,
drew the Chancellor more and more toward
the lesser court, and Catherine. In this he was
not alone.

From the first weeks of his arrival in Russia Sir Charles Hanbury-Williams had paid court to Catherine. In his despatches he wrote that the health of the Empress was bad, and that he believed, in the event of her death, power would rest with Catherine rather than with Peter; and Catherine was, he found, well disposed towards England. Apart from his recognition of her strength of character, Sir Charles found much in Catherine to attract him; and the attraction was mutual, although based, perhaps, rather on intellectual affinity than on anything else. It was, in fact, one of the secretaries attached to the staff of the English minister, a young Polish prince, Stanislas Poniatowski, who now became Catherine's lover. But intercourse with those two experienced diplomatists, Bestúzhev and Hanbury-Williams, must have been a further step in Catherine's education. So the game was played behind the back of the Empress. Bestúzhev and Hanbury-Williams, each jealous of the influence of the other with Catherine, but each recognizing her importance for the future as she recognized theirs. And, for Catherine, the additional pleasure of a new lover, the Polish prince, elegant, cultivated, with distinguished manners, who could be used, and who was used as an intermediary by all three of the players of the game, and by their friends.

Yet Bestúzhev might well have regained some of the influence he had lost with Elizabeth but for his invincible dislike and distrust of France. He refused to recognize that, in view of the diplomatic revolution which had brought together Austria and France against Prussia, the obvious course for Russia to pursue as an ally of Austria and opponent of Prussia was an approach to France. It was a course that was being urged on the Empress by the Shuvalovs, always inclined to France. They triumphed. In January, 1757, Russia declared her adherence to the treaty of Versailles, as negotiated by Austria and France.

The following August a Russian army under General Stephan Apraxim crossed the Vistula and entered East Prussia. On the 30th of the month they defeated the Prussian army at Gross Jägerndorf. What had been looked upon, quite erroneously as was now proved, as a body of half-trained inexperienced troops, had triumphed over forces renowned throughout Europe for their military efficiency. To Frederick the shock was considerable; none the less so because his armies had already during the past year been hard pressed by the coalition forces of Austria and France. Yet for the time being the Russian victory seemed to bring little result. After remaining in East Prussia throughout September, chiefly occupied in marching and counter-marching his men, Apraxim withdrew once more behind the Vistula, having made no attempt to follow up his success or even to consolidate it. From the military point of view the obvious explanation was that offered by the

General in his own defence: the difficulty of
bringing up supplies. This difficulty was compli-
cated by another. Apraxim's army was composed
of two sets of forces widely different from one
another. He had his infantry whose training and
discipline had astonished Frederick for one. But
he also had his horsemen, mainly Cossacks, terrible
to their opponents in their onslaught, nevertheless
ever freebooters, not easily susceptible to control,
and apt to quit the main body of the army
according to their own desires. This portion of his
forces certainly began, after the battle, to melt
away. Apraxim may well have thought that as
a commander, he had no choice but to retire for
the winter into Russian territory. The withdrawal, however, had far-reaching repercussions
within Russia.

In September the Empress was at Tsarskoe Selo.
Attending Mass one morning at the parish church,
she was seized with an apoplectic fit. Instantly the
rumour spread that her seizure was the direct
result of her anger and anxiety caused by the
retreat. Available evidence points to there being
no connection whatever between the two happenings; and the war council in St. Petersburg had,
in fact, with the consent of the Empress, themselves ordered the withdrawal a fortnight earlier.
The point of the rumour, however, was that the
withdrawal was connected with the name of
Bestúzhev. He, whispered his opponents and
particularly the Shuvalovs, had seduced Apraxim,

the latter willingly consenting to play the part of a traitor. And, so the whispers continued, the Grand-duchess had also been privy to the proceedings.

It was, to say the least, highly improbable that Bestúzhev, whose lifelong policy had been opposition to Prussia, would have thus deliberately played into the hands of Frederick, nor does it seem likely that Apraxim would have so sacrificed his military reputation. For that matter, too, it was the Grand-duke who was, as the new French ambassador called him, the ape of Frederick, not Catherine. Nevertheless, Apraxim was undoubtedly involved in the understanding that existed between the Grand-duchess and the Chancellor, with the English minister playing his part. And not he only. Among others, the Russian minister-plenipotentiary in Stockholm, Count Nikita Panin, whose father, an Italian of Lucca, had been lieutenant-general to Peter the Great, had entered into correspondence with both the Grand-duchess and Sir Charles Hanbury-Williams.

The stay of the last-named in Russia was, however, drawing to a close. In the autumn he took ship from Cronstadt leaving behind him a state of affairs of which the Shuvalovs and the court camarilla which they directed took instant advantage.

As the Empress in some measure recovered her health, one piece of evidence after another was placed before her; and early in 1758 orders were given for the arrest of Bestúzhev and Apraxim. The charge was of conspiracy with the Grand-duchess to withdraw the army in order to have it ready for a coup d'état on behalf of Catherine in the event of the death of the Empress. This was a far more explicable charge than that of having endeavoured to aid Frederick; and also far more dangerous to the persons concerned. No one was in a position to know better than the Empress just what part the army could play in the matter of succession to the crown. Nor can there be any doubt that the Chancellor and the Grand-duchess in conjunction with the English minister had been skating on very thin ice indeed. Now came accusations and counter-accusations, intrigue and counter-intrigue. Bestúzhev was not helped by the share taken in the proceedings by the newly arrived ambassador from France, Paul de l'Hôpital, who was active against the unfortunate Chancellor. It was an action more understandable from him than the similar course followed by Count Esterhazy, who represented Austria, a country always supported by Bestúzhev. Finally, in these happenings, Johanna von Anhalt-Zerbst once more appeared on the horizon. Johanna, a widow since 1747, had a short time before arrived in Paris and in the last years of her life was again trying her hand at the diplomatic game. No more success than before attended her efforts; she died in 1759, a poor woman, a disappointed woman, only cheered before the end by a few presents which Catherine contrived to send her.

In the meantime Catherine, Bestúzhev and Apraxim had to face the situation. Apraxim was condemned to death as a traitor. His sentence was, however, commuted to imprisonment, during which, in the following year, he died. Bestúzhev, confronted by his accusers, protested his innocence. His enemies asked that torture might be used to extract a confession. This the Empress refused to allow. She contented herself with depriving the Chancellor of his office. He was succeeded by the Vice-chancellor and former Chamberlain, Count Michael Vorontsov, not a man of outstanding character. There remained the Grand-duchess to be dealt with.

Catherine had not at any time deceived herself as to the danger inherent in what she was doing. And that danger, she knew well, was the greater because of the rapid worsening of relations between herself and her husband. Whatever she, and others, might think of Peter, whatever his weaknesses, he remained her husband and no less heir to the throne of Russia, an inheritance that would, in the belief of many, be very shortly entered upon. Now, enamoured of the most recent of his mistresses, Elizabeth Vorontsov, niece of the newly appointed Chancellor, he was openly evincing dislike of the wife who despised him, and he may already have been thinking, as he was certainly to think a little later, in terms of divorce for the one and marriage with the other.

Under such conditions, a slip might well have sealed Catherine's fate and she later admitted that she had always had fears as to what might have happened to her during the lifetime of the Empress. She would have been unnatural indeed not to be shaken when, Sir Charles Hanbury-Williams gone, Bestúzhev in disgrace, she was finally summoned into the presence of the Empress —and of her husband—to account for her actions. Her memoirs give a description of the scene. The hour was midnight and the place the imperial bed-chamber—that long room with its three great windows and its dressing tables spread with glittering, golden toilet appointments. Catherine, advancing, flung herself at the feet of the Empress, protesting her loyalty, while the Grand-duke stood by with, as she wrote, a malignant look on his face. Bestúzhev had destroyed the correspondence between Catherine and himself. But other letters had been found and brought to the room, incriminating letters. Despite these, despite what Elizabeth had been told, despite the unconcealed animosity of the Grand-duke, Catherine triumphed. She left the bedroom at three in the morning, still a free woman, to spend the following days in retirement in her own rooms, consoling herself, as she afterwards remarked, by turning over the leaves of the first volume of the *Encyclopædia*. When, finally, she again emerged into public, she was able to say that she found the

Empress somewhat softened towards her. The opinion of de l'Hôpital, expressed in a despatch written a little later, was that Elizabeth, a sick and ageing woman, had made up her mind not to worry any more about the conduct of either the Grand-duke or the Grand-duchess. One thing she could and did do. She kept them both lamentably short of money.

In these last days of her life, Elizabeth must, in respect of her heir and his wife, both chosen by herself, have been a yet more deeply disappointed and disillusioned woman. But in one matter her determination did not falter. Often irritated by the lack of support on the part of her allies, France and Austria, angry at their dissensions, it was the will of Elizabeth that her army should continue until the might of Prussia should, as she hoped, be quelled.

In the spring of 1758 the Russian army once more crossed the Prussian frontier, and although this time Frederick triumphed at the battle of Zorndorf, the victory was nullified by a loss of men which he could ill afford; and no less by the skill with which the Russian infantry were withdrawn, the troops whom Frederick had learned to dread, not only for their numbers but for the steadfastness with which they could fight. Against them he could set his own men, trained to a degree of military efficiency as perhaps no army before them had ever been. But, even with what was to all intents and purposes a system of kidnapping,

Frederick could not compete with his opponents in man-power. At the same time the Russian irregular horse and Cossacks, under no such discipline as were the infantry, were once more terrorizing the countryside. When, in 1759, the Russians, after another stay in winter quarters, entered Pomerania and inflicted a decisive defeat upon the Prussians at Kunersdorf, Frederick fell into despair. It was one of the moments in his career when, believing all lost, he contemplated the possibility of suicide. The weakness of the Russian position was, however, what could have been and had been, brought forward in defence of Apraxim: the difficulty of supplies which forced withdrawal during the winter months. So it happened again after Kunersdorf, that Frederick had some respite.

It was the events of the following year, 1760, that impressed upon Prussia and its king the danger in which they stood. In the spring advance the Russians this time crossed the Oder; and parties of Cossacks, pressing on, reached and raided Berlin. The situation grew worse when, during the winter, the invading army at last did not go behind the Vistula but remained in Pomerania.

Throughout the following year Frederick, pressed on all sides, believed himself again and again to be at his last gasp. His one ally, England, where George III had succeeded George II, was not prepared to help him even to the extent of sending a fleet to the Baltic, nor had that ally ever broken off diplomatic relations with his enemy, Russia. His best hope lay in the dispositions of his opponents. The energies of France were primarily directed towards the struggle with her particular enemy, England; on the high seas; in India; in North America. There was, too, a lack of co-ordination between the Russian and Austrian armies. Nevertheless, it seemed as the year 1761 drew to its close, that when, in the following spring, Russia should once more advance, with Pomerania as her base, it would be the end of Frederick. But before the next year had well opened, the entire situation had changed.

All the summer the Empress had been at Peterhof, a very sick woman. In October she came back to the capital, and was installed in the Winter Palace. That palace had been since 1754 once more in the process of rebuilding, again under the direction of Rastrelli, and was even now not quite finished. But the Empress never saw the completion of the work. In December she had another apoplectic seizure. It proved to be the last and the fatal one. She died, fifty-two years of age, on the twenty-third of the month (4 January, 1762, N.S.).

Chapter Three

The Empress Consort

THE death of the Empress might well, in the opinion of more than one of her contemporaries, have precipitated an immediate crisis. So nervous had been the Chancellor Vorontsov that he, always a slight, unmeritable man, had deliberately absented himself from court during the last few days of the life of Elizabeth, pleading illness. He, like others, knew that, during the time of long anticipation of the end, many schemes, other than those which had come into the full light of day, had been hatching. For some little time now it had been no close secret that the intention of the Grand-duke had been, once he became his own master, to divorce and banish his wife, declare the boy Paul a bastard; and marry Elizabeth Vorontsov. But each figure which stood near the throne had in his or her turn been the subject of suggested conspiracy. The Shuvalovs, for their part, were well known to have a plan whereby Paul, instead of being deprived of his succession, was himself to be placed on the throne, and not only his father, but his mother likewise, sent into banishment.

Information of the existence of this plot had been conveyed to Catherine by Sir Charles

Hanbury-Williams, who had added that in his opinion the matter was sufficiently serious; and that the Grand-duchess had better look to her own safety. On that point Catherine was wholly of the same mind as Sir Charles. But, she had told him, her ideas for the future did not include any project of seeking sanctuary at the court of King George of England. Rather, she intended to keep herself, and her son, safe—in Russia; and always she would try to conciliate her enemies in preference to alienating them. Now Sir Charles lay in his tomb in Westminster Abbey, for he had not long survived his retreat from Russia; and Peter Shuvalov was a dying man—he survived his Empress only ten days. He had been the leading person in the family and the group; and with his illness and death the danger arising out of a move by his party, danger which threatened Catherine as well as her husband, receded. The possibility of trouble from other quarters remained; and among other warnings one had reached Catherine on the night of 9 December (20 December, N.S.), when there had appeared in her bedchamber a young woman who was to become one of her closest friends and admirers. The lady was the Princess Daschkov, the eighteen-year-old sister of Peter's mistress, Elizabeth Vorontsov; in which relationship and as niece of the Chancellor she was in a position to collect a good deal of information. She now announced to Catherine that plans were afoot which threatened the latter's position,

possibly even her life. To that Catherine replied
in the same vein as she had replied to Sir Charles
Hanbury-Williams. She was, she told her young
friend, quite content to remain calm and to await
what fortune should send her.

Five nights later Catherine stood by her husband's side in the death chamber of the Empress;
and from that death chamber the senior senator
stepped forth to proclaim the accession to the
throne, as Peter III, of Elizabeth's nephew and
heir. Despite the disturbed and turgid movements
which had played so big a part in the background
of the last years of Elizabeth, all had gone smoothly
—for the moment. Peter and Catherine became
Emperor—that imperial title adopted by the first
Peter—and Empress Consort of Russia with no
voice raised against them; but with every eye
fixed upon them, judging them, appraising them.

Outside Russia, one person at least must have
felt a great lightening of the spirit, when informed
by his messengers that the Empress of Russia,
whose end had for so long been anticipated, had
now at last succumbed. And when, early in
February, emissaries from the newly acceded
Emperor of Russia arrived in Breslau with proposals for peace, Frederick of Prussia was justified
in his belief that all would now be well with him.

That Peter would make peace was a foregone
conclusion; and a treaty favourable to Russia
might well have been acquiesced in. Many of
those in the immediate royal circle had no desire

to continue with the war, and it is more than probable that Catherine might have been numbered with these. The difference between the outlook of this group and that of Peter was, however, quickly apparent. Russia was, as the former saw clearly, in a very strong position to demand good terms, in the face of her successes in the field; with her troops occupying East Prussia and part of Pomerania and her ally, Austria, on Frederick's flank in Silesia. In London the Russian Ambassador told the Prime Minister, Lord Bute, that Russia would certainly not evacuate the conquered provinces and would claim, as a right, final possession of East Prussia. It was indeed known, if not then, at least a little later, that Frederick would have been willing to give up East Prussia were he to be given in exchange, and guaranteed, the secure possession of Saxony. But when put forward that suggestion was disallowed by the other interested powers. In his negotiations with Peter, however, the King of Prussia had it all his own way.

On 24 April (5 May, N.S.) the Emperor of Russia signed a document which restored to Prussia all the territory occupied and held in recent years by Russia; with a clause providing for close alliance and amity between the two countries.

The public announcement of what was in effect complete surrender to Prussia was followed by celebrations offered to the people, in St. Peters-

burg, in Moscow and elsewhere, that they, too,
might rejoice. As was usual, street tableaux were
included and one of these displayed to the inhabitants of St. Petersburg a representation of Russia
and Prussia meeting together in love and unity.
The Russian populace were hardly likely to have
taken an interest in, or know anything of, foreign
policy. The ministers, and others in a position to
judge of what had happened and was happening,
were deeply offended.

Yet, almost at the same moment, Peter took
another step, one concerning internal affairs,
which should, under normal conditions, have
ensured his popularity with the nobility and the
gentry. In the month of May he issued an edict
which released the upper classes from their
remaining obligations to do state service. In so
doing he pulled the linch-pin from the scheme
of social structure which had been laid down by
Peter the Great. This linch-pin had, it must be
said, already considerably loosened. Peter's act
gave impetus to a course of events that was already
in train, and, being unchecked, was ultimately to
end in catastrophe.

Peter the Great had developed the idea of a
state in which service should be due from all.
Thus he had created, or, more truly, reconstructed, a standing army and navy and a standing
civil administration combined with a court
officialdom, in one or other of which all men of the
upper classes—a term practically conterminous

with that of landowners—were compelled to serve and to be educated, as of obligation, for that purpose. At the same time any one, however humble his origin, might, having entered on one of these employments, climb upwards through the fourteen grades into which the civil administration was divided, or attain officer rank in the army or the navy. The first eight grades for civilian and all officer rank carried with them entry into the gentry and landowning class of society, with, in appropriate cases, titles of nobility. Thus, while this class was greatly, even enormously, augmented it might also be claimed that membership thereof depended not upon birth but upon service. And to a great degree this was so. But the scheme had many weak points, not omitting the influence of wealth and position and, above all, of favouritism.

Two of the weakest points, carrying with them seeds of future trouble, stood out clearly. What had been done was to reorganize a bureaucracy which was already in existence, and upon which the rulers of Russia had always been dependent. As reconstituted, this bureaucracy, subject to no check save that of the crown and its delegates, became more powerful than ever before.

At the same time the swelling of the ranks of the privileged class implied a corresponding increase in the number of serf-owners. It was small wonder that the desire of this class, not excluding those newly admitted to it, was to secure further privileges and to ease their obligations; and that once the iron hand of Peter the Great had been removed they should have set themselves to do both. Moreover, while their own position had been thus improving, that of the peasants who were largely their serfs, and to a great extent that of other workers also, such as those in industry, had been deteriorating.

Slavery, in the strictest sense of the word, to which a man might be brought by such factors as captivity or crime or debt, existed in the old Russia which was Muscovy as elsewhere in medieval Europe. But the wholesale transformation of free men into serfs, which brought about the condition of affairs as it was in 1762, had its origin in ideas which, when originally promulgated, had seemed reasonable; yet held the seeds of extreme evil. Fundamental among these ideas was that which insisted upon the tying of the agricultural worker or peasant in especial—although again other classes of workers were involved—to one particular estate or one particular master. That master might be the state or the crown, for there were many crown peasants, or an individual landowner or employer, great or small.

Such a tying up had been conceived of as a necessity. From the time when Russia had begun to expand under the rule of Moscow, it had been clear that the prosperity of the country, perhaps even its survival, depended upon the efficient working of agriculture. Here authority had found itself confronted by a double problem. On the one hand was the grave shortage of workers on the land. This was by no means a problem peculiar to Russia. It was one with which other countries, including, particularly in the sixteenth century, England, had had to grapple. In Russia the difficulties were increased, on the one hand, by the immensity of the country, the great stretches of land requiring workers, and, on the other, by certain characteristics of the peasant in Russia. He was, as John Maynard has pointed out in his sympathetic study, entitled *The Russian Peasant*, a peasant in whom the nomad survived; a man who, with much of the Asiatic in him, had instinctively a taste for being always on the move. The vast Russian forests, the great Russian plains which rolled on to commingle with the forests and plains of Asia, with only the break in one spot made by the comparatively low range of the Ural mountains, offered plenty of room in which to wander. If the soil in one spot should prove unproductive, or were the surroundings unattractive, nothing was easier for a man, for a family, for a group of families, even amounting to a whole village, to move on elsewhere. The landowners, in their turn, were not slow to secure necessary labour, either by the offer of better conditions than prevailed in other places or more simply by a process of kidnapping.

Hence the story of the growth of serfdom is very largely the story of a series of edicts, spread over many years, which at first limited, and then finally prohibited, any freedom of movement whatsoever for agricultural workers and, to a greater extent as time went on, for other workers also. By the time Peter the Great had come to the throne a considerable section of the peasants had lost their ancient right of changing their masters at will, once a year, at the date approximating to Michaelmas; did they run away, they were reckoned as criminals; in short, for many, a condition of human bondage had been reached. Next, the edicts of Peter himself, while imposing compulsory service on all, had at the same time bound the peasants more closely to their masters; by the poll tax, which had the effect of linking together the masters—who, from 1730 onwards, were made responsible for its collection—with the state against the peasants; by the passport system, by which a peasant could not pass the boundary of his master's estate without a written permission, only given to the head of a family; and, above all, by the quickening up of the process by which those who, till now, had enjoyed varying degrees of personal freedom—there had always been an infinite number of grades of peasantdom—had had that freedom gradually pared down until all alike were reduced to the common level of bondage. The lowest point had been reached when the peasant-serf could, whether under conditions or no, be bought and sold. Here again the underlying theory had been that since the land was useless without the worker, the latter must go with the land, whether it was a case of sale or a gift from the crown for services rendered. But in practice, in spite of legislation, serfs, during the eighteenth century, could be, and frequently were, sold as individuals, not as attached to property.

Then came the edict of May, 1762, destroying what remained of the balanced obligations of each class as Peter the Great had conceived of them. Once the upper strata of society had been freed from compulsory service, justice and logic then required that the class below should likewise be freed from serving under conditions over which they had no control, conditions which left them at the mercy of their masters; conditions which might vary, as writers on the subject have shown, from being tolerable, save always for the negation of personal freedom, to something that was unspeakably bad, according as the individual master was good, bad or indifferent.

And even, in 1762, under Peter III, logic and justice did have something to say. There arose a rumour that a second edict, one that would at least have given the peasants and their fellows some sort of freedom, had been prepared and had been suppressed. Whether this was so or not, that rumour bore fruit in the future.

What, or who, had suggested to Peter the issue of the May edict, must be largely a matter for surmise. As an attempt, if it was so meant, to gain the sympathy of the upper classes, it was entirely unsuccessful, holding nothing wherewith to counterbalance the distrust already excited by what had been seen of his character as Grand-duke; a distrust which during the five months of his reign had been increasing by leaps and bounds.

The nature of the pact with Frederick had been a primary cause of offence. The same unwisdom, the same infatuation for his idol, had moved the Emperor to antagonize two groups in the community whom he could ill afford to antagonize. In the very first weeks of his succession he had offended the dignitaries of the church, and others with them, by his neglect of the ecclesiastical ceremonies that counted for so much in the life of Russia; and to neglect he had added scoffing and jeering. His next step threatened the very life of the Orthodox Church, for he proposed that it should reform itself so as to approximate to the Lutheran model, while all its property was to be secularized.

Similarly the army had been threatened. Long since Peter had played, in so far as he had been allowed, the part of a Prussian drill-master, with such soldiers as he had at his command, and in particular the regiment of guards drawn from his own principality of Holstein. Now he would have the entire Russian army submitted to such drill masters and so Prussianized in good earnest.

Hasty and ill-advised, such moves must in any event have been resented. The resentment had behind it all the scorn felt for, all the apprehen-

sions excited by, the antics of a ruler who, intoxi-
cated with power, was seen to be vainer, more
arrogant and, above all, more unstable than before.

In the background stood Catherine. Onlookers
were agreed that the Emperor seldom, if ever,
consulted her on affairs. They saw also that where
the personal relationship was concerned the breach
between the two was complete. Even while the
Emperor redoubled his attentions to Elizabeth
Vorontsov, he was treating Catherine, not only in
private but in public, with unashamed rudeness
and even brutality. Divorce from the latter and
marriage with the former was now, everyone
suspected, at hand. Those watching Catherine,
including the representatives of foreign courts,
noted her dignity when subjected to open slights
and insolence. New arrivals noted too, what had
long been perceived by those in proximity to
her, the impression conveyed of character and of
ability. Outside Russia, the King of Prussia,
writing to the English envoy in St. Petersburg,
recommended that he should take Catherine's
opinion on affairs, whenever he deemed it necessary or desirable. Frederick had, in fact, already
long since summed up the importance of the
woman whom he had helped to place where she
was. He was far from being the only one to do
so. In the background to which her husband had
consigned her, Catherine received ministers and
ambassadors. And, to set against Peter's mistress,
she had a new lover. He was Gregori Orlov, one

71

of the five sons of a former governor of Novgorod;
handsome, able and young; twenty-eight years of
age against thirty-five years of the Empress.

So the weeks, the uneasy weeks, passed; and
matters went from bad to worse. Peter's ever-
growing infatuation for Frederick and for Prussia
was marked by his constant references to his idol
on all occasions. When, in the early summer, he
received from Frederick what he had long coveted,
the Order of the Black Eagle, he celebrated the
event by a day-long cannonade from the fortress
of St. Peter and St. Paul; and announced that
henceforth he would wear this order and no other.
Elsewhere manifestations of his folly and his irres-
ponsibility and his viciousness increased daily.
It was said openly that the Chancellor had begged
to be allowed to resign and go into private life.

The end came quickly. The Russian crown
had suffered violence before. It was about to
suffer it again. During the month of June Peter
was at Oranienbaum, amusing himself with his
fiddle and, as ever, with military exercises.
Catherine was at Peterhof occupying the pavilion
in the park known as Mon Plaisir. Thence she
came over to Oranienbaum on a visit to her
husband; and at an entertainment given for them
at another great house, they appeared together for
the last time.

It was probably at this point that Peter was
warned that mischief was afoot. He took no notice
at the moment. But for him the end was very

near. There was, indeed, a conspiracy brewing.

The actors in the plot were all of one mind in that they were determined that Peter must be removed from the throne. It was as to what should happen after he had gone that they differed. The Princess Daschkov, who, according to her own account, was one of the principals, seems to have been of those who wanted the crown for the seven-year-old Grand-duke Paul, with a regency for Catherine. The princess had, it was said, been the one to persuade Count Nikita Panin, the former diplomat—correspondent of Catherine and Sir Charles Hanbury-Williams, to join the conspirators. But probably little persuasion was required. The Count had been brought back from Stockholm the previous year, to be made tutor and governor to the little Grand-duke; an office which gave him ample opportunity to survey the situation. He now joined those who proposed to place the boy on the throne, with his mother as regent.

But others were involved; notably Catherine's lover, Gregori Orlov, intent upon the aggrandizement of Catherine. With Gregori were his eldest brother, Alexis, perhaps the ablest of the family, and a younger brother, Theodore. It must be added, that apart from the personal relationship between Gregori and Catherine, the former and his family stood out among that section of the nobility who, in the new growth of Slav national feeling, most resented the threatened Germanization of Russia at the hands of her ruler. From

the practical point of view the Orlovs had one
supreme advantage. They were in touch with
the army; and it was with the support of the
army that they acted.

In the early hours of 28 June (9 July, N.S.),
Alexis Orlov arrived at Mon Plaisir and asked for
Catherine to be wakened. To her he communi-
cated that the moment for action had come and
must be seized. Otherwise all might be in danger
since it was known that information was reaching
Peter. There was no delay. Catherine, under
the escort of Alexis, left for St. Petersburg—one
tale subsequently told in the capital was that she
got out of a window of the pavilion. On the road
the travellers were met by Gregori Orlov, who
took them to the guards' barracks standing at the
approach to the capital. At the barracks
Catherine received the homage of the three
principal regiments. But there was still no time
to waste; and the procession, now augmented
by companies of the guards, went on to enter
St. Petersburg and turn into the Nevsky Prospect,
making for the church of Our Lady of Kazan,
the church in which seventeen years earlier
the marriage of Peter and Catherine had been
celebrated. It was not yet nine in the morning
when the edifice was reached. But messages
had gone out. On the entrance steps—the events
of the day were subsequently recorded in a series
of paintings—was standing the Archbishop of
Novgorod; and with him a crowd of clergy and

nobles. And there, too, was the little Grand-duke Paul with Count Panin. A Spanish diplomat, whose dwelling was close to the church, reported that so great had been the hurry that the child, when seen seated by his governor in the carriage which brought them to the church, was still wearing his nightcap. Nor, according to the same informant, were all the soldiers fully dressed. But fourteen thousand of them closed round the church as Catherine entered, to hear herself proclaimed by the Archbishop as Empress of Russia; with the rider that her son, the Grand-duke Paul, was her natural heir and successor.

In that moment, as Brückner has pointed out, Peter's fate was sealed. In that moment, it might be added, some at least of those present must have become aware that matters were not going to take precisely the course they had in mind.

From the church the whole party went on to the Winter Palace. Within and without the building, now almost complete, was a great crowd—more officials, more clergy, more of the army and a concourse of the people of the capital. To the officials and clergy Catherine read a manifesto; then, stepping on to the balcony in response to the shouts of the crowd gathered there, she received a tumultuous welcome. Peter was about to pay very dear for the wilful alienation of every section of society that counted and who could almost, at their will, rouse the populace.

Busy at Oranienbaum drilling his Holstein

Guards, the Emperor seems to have known nothing all that day of what was happening in his capital. He learned something of the story the following day, almost fortuitously, from a peasant. He then decided to go over to Peterhof and did so, to find, as he had been forewarned, that Catherine was not there. Some hours of bewilderment followed. Peter had with him Vorontsov, Alexander Shuvalov and the senior senator, Prince Troubezkoi. He could, he believed, count on his Holsteiners. The Chancellor, Shuvalov and Troubezkoi decided to make their way to the capital, to ascertain what was really happening. Peter never saw any of them again. He himself, it was determined, should go to Cronstadt, where it was hoped he would have the protection of the fleet. But he never reached that fortress. He was at Oranienbaum when Catherine came back to Peterhof in the early hours of the first day of July (12 July, N.S.).

It was an amazing return. The party had left the capital late the previous evening; Catherine, mounted on a white horse, riding at the head of her troops. She wore uniform, a man's uniform, borrowed from a young lieutenant. Her hat was wreathed with oak-leaves. Those who watched remarked on her fine horsemanship, the horsemanship perfected in her early days in Russia; on the manner in which she held herself; on her triumphant countenance. At her side, also in male uniform, rode the Princess Daschkov. And so, in the summer night, they came to Peterhof. Within twenty-four hours Peter, fetched with Elizabeth Vorontsov from Oranienbaum by Alexis Orlov, had signed his abdication and had been removed, still in the custody of Alexis, to Ropsha, a pretty little château standing in its park in the little village of the same name, a few miles to the south of St. Petersburg.

How this struck a contemporary is recorded by one of the letter writers of England. Information about the events occurring in Russia inevitably travelled slowly. On 31 July, Horace Walpole heard at Strawberry Hill that the Emperor of Russia had been dethroned. On 10 August, he was able to write to George Montagu:

'What do you say to a czarina mounting horse and marching at the head of 14,000 men to dethrone her husband? Yet she is not the only Virago in the country. The conspiracy was conducted by the sister of the czar's mistress, a heroine under twenty! They have no fewer than two czars now in coops, that is, supposing these gentle damsels have murdered neither of them. . . . Here's room for meditation ev'n to madness. . . .

'This is the fourth czarina you and I have seen —to be sure as historians we have not passed our time ill. Mrs. Anne Pitt who, I suspect, envies a heroine of twenty, says the czarina has only robbed Peter to pay Paul!'

Mrs. Anne Pitt was the fifty-year-old, sharp-tongued, eccentric—very eccentric indeed, poor lady, as she grew older—sister of William Pitt.

The second of the two rulers, to whom Walpole alluded, was the unfortunate young man who, as a babe, had been known as Ivan VI. He had been barely a year old when he had been hurried away by guards at the command of Elizabeth, the day she had seized the throne. Ever since he had been kept a close prisoner in the island fortress of Schlüsselberg—Peter the Great's key fortress at the source of the Neva as it issued from Lake Ladoga—a pathetic, half-forgotten, but still living figure.

In the matter of the other Emperor, who had, indeed, occupied the throne, they, or some of them, took no chances. Walpole's surmise that even as he wrote Peter might no longer be alive was correct.

Orlov, his soldiers and companions, carrying the Emperor with them, had reached Ropsha on 30 June (11 July, N.S.). Peter was then said to have been ill in mind and body. It is certain that doctors were called in. A few days passed. On the night of 5 July (16 July, N.S.) Peter died. Before burial in the monastery to which the coffin was consigned, his body was exhibited. For this course of action the reasons were obvious. The Russian authorities knew all about the possibility of resuscitated claimants to the throne.

The various narratives concerning the fate of
the unfortunate man have been collected and set
forth by the historian of his reign. But even so,
Mr. Nisbet Bain has reached no absolute conclusion. The statement of Orlov was simple
enough. The Emperor, he reported, had met
his death in a drunken scuffle after supper;
and, added Orlov, neither he nor anyone else
remembered what had actually occurred. There
was never any real doubt, either then or later, that
murder had been done. How it was accomplished,
who were involved, and, above all, the part, if
any, played by Catherine, remain matters for
speculation.

Many years afterwards, one night in May, 1804,
when Catherine herself had lain for some years in
her grave, the Princess Daschkov, who had survived
her mistress, told a friend, the Englishwoman,
Catherine Wilmot, to whom the princess was in
the habit of reading every evening extracts from
Catherine's correspondence, sometimes to the
boredom of her friend—she came in again with a
pile of letters, wrote Miss Wilmot, with a touch
of weariness—that the murder had been con-
nived at by almost every man in St. Petersburg,
and that even before this his rooms had always
been guarded because of known hatreds for
him. His wife, continued the princess, had
often remarked on this state of affairs and had
added that as far as her own safety was concerned no guards were necessary. The state-

ment probably sums up, not badly, the respective positions occupied by Peter and Catherine in the world of St. Petersburg and Moscow, a small world, indeed, compared with the great stretches of the rest of Russia, but, in the matter of dethroning and enthroning a sovereign, the only world that counted.

In England, Horace Walpole, writing to the Countess of Ailesbury after news of the death had been confirmed, told her that while there was no question that Peter had been murdered, public opinion was much divided as to the instrument. Some thought it was the wife; others said it was the Archbishop of Novgorod. The view of the writer was that while the Archbishop would doubtless, like other priests, think assassination a less affront to Heaven than three Lutheran churches, the instigator of the crime was the lady for whom, among a variety of other titles, none of them complimentary, that he gave her, he coined the name of Catherine Slay-Czar.

Frederick of Prussia, being informed that the Emperor had died of colic, remarked that every-one knew the nature of the colic. A few days later he wrote to the Queen of Sweden that Catherine, in her ambition, had risked all and had not scrupled to poison her husband. To Prince Henry of Prussia he said that the blood of the grandson of Peter the Great cried out against her. But all Frederick's correspondence during these weeks when news was filtering through from Russia

testifies to his perturbation: his fear of a reversal
of the policy Peter had pursued towards Prussia:
a declaration that the treaty of alliance was null
and void. Twenty years later, when he and
Catherine had long been correspondents, the
King of Prussia was, or said he was, of another
opinion. He told the ambassador, Ségur, on
his way from France to take up his post in
St. Petersburg, that personally he had never
held Catherine to blame. In his opinion, she, a
foreigner in the land, on the point of being
divorced and shut up for life, had thrown herself into the hands of the Orlovs. And even so,
he thought she had known nothing of the intended
murder; and that, left to herself, she would have
kept Peter alive; partly because she believed he
could be made harmless, partly because she saw
or thought she saw the effect that putting him
out of the world would have on public opinion,
both inside and outside Russia. The Orlovs,
continued Frederick to the ambassador, had been
more clear-sighted than she. They had seen that
Peter must die. As for the Princess Daschkov,
that young lady, in the judgment of the King of
Prussia, had been in the whole business nothing
more than the silly fly buzzing on the wheel. The
change of opinion may well have derived from
later information received. It may equally have
been affected by the political relations between
himself and the Empress.

There remains the imponderable factor of

human nature. Catherine's own memoirs can only be read as those of a woman desiring to justify herself to herself—an attitude of mind that must always be taken into consideration in any estimate of Catherine—and to the world. And this is particularly relevant to all she wrote of her husband and her life with him. Yet, according to her lights, she had, during at least the early years of her marriage, done her best for Peter. At no time in her life did she show herself cruel for cruelty's sake. Rather the contrary. Her correspondence, her recorded utterances, her manipulation of events in moments of crisis, all go to show her mind was fixed on a future in which she would be the predominant figure. This may have meant nothing more than that she was sure that as between her husband and herself she would lead in all that was of importance. But as the situation developed, and she and her supporters perceived the real danger conveyed by the threat of divorce, her very coolness of judgment, her self-mastery, harnessed to her ambition, may have told as much against the wretched Peter as the passion of another and a different woman might have done.

Chapter Four

The Empress

F. W. MAITLAND, writing of Scottish affairs as they appeared in the sixteenth century, remarked:

'A king shall be kidnapped and a king shall be murdered, as of old—it is the custom of the country. What is new is that far-sighted men all over Europe . . . should take an interest in these barbarous deeds, this customary turmoil.'

The words might have been written of Russian affairs two hundred years later.

On 7 July (18 July, N.S.), 1762, Catherine issued an edict. Therein she announced to the people of Russia that her husband, the Emperor Peter III, had died suddenly in the course of an attack of the illness to which he had long been subject. At the same time she made it amply clear that she regarded herself as his successor. Neither here, nor in the earliest manifesto issued at the Winter Palace, did she even hint that she might rule on behalf of her seven-year-old son.

The idea of a regency, an idea which had been in the mind of more than one of her supporters, found no response in the mind of Catherine.

83

Were the customary law of succession to be observed the boy Paul was at this moment undoubtedly the true successor to the throne of Russia, unless the claim of the unhappy Ivan VI was to be considered.

Observance of the usual law of succession had not, however, been a conspicuous element in the history of the Russian crown in the years gone by. This, in itself, was in one sense a help to Catherine. What she was now doing, others, and some of them of her own sex, had done before her. And she could claim, as others had claimed before her, that she succeeded by virtue of her connections by marriage with the royal house of Romanov. The quasi-mystic sentiment behind such a claim was a powerful one. The assembly of the land, which, in 1613 had chosen the first of the Romanov line as Tsar, had done so because of his connections by marriage with the royal family of Rurik. As the great-nephew of the wife of Ivan the Terrible, the last of the Rurik dynasty, Michael Romanov, of a family of noble but not exalted rank, had been held in some sort to represent the ancient line. So, too, Peter the Great, never nominating his heir as he had by his own edict intended to do—that law was a dead letter from the first—had been succeeded by his widow Catherine the Lithuanian. Now another Catherine claimed in her turn to succeed Peter III; Peter who had been hurried out of the world, if not by her connivance at least as the work of her friends and supporters. And, as was written of another country in another age, far-sighted men all over Europe took an interest in the deed; and the possible results.

In England the manifesto, when it reached the country, was given considerable prominence in the news sheets. A piece of 'honest impudence in modern majesty,' was Horace Walpole's comment; and he expressed the opinion that the title of a princess of Anhalt-Zerbst to the crown was not likely to appeal to the good Muscovite. In common with many another onlooker, he did not give Catherine power of continuance for many months.

That there was danger, many in St. Petersburg and in Moscow were well aware. There was reason for hurrying on the preparation for the great act of coronation which should set the seal on the earlier proclamations. In September the court left the new capital for the old. The ceremony took place on the 22nd of that month.

The figure who on that September day stood on the customary platform in the nave of the Chapel of the Assumption within the Kremlin, wearing a dress of cloth of silver, with trimmings of the imperial ermine, was, as the English Envoy, the Earl of Buckinghamshire, who came to St. Petersburg in 1762, set down in his memoranda, that of a woman of scarcely more than middle height, with features that were nothing out of the ordinary. But the glossy chestnut-coloured hair massed under the high jewelled Russian crown was beautiful, and the blue eyes beneath were remarkable for their brightness. The head, too, was well poised on a long neck. It was the carriage of the head that was seen to lend dignity to the entire figure; a dignity that was in keeping with the impression received by onlookers of pride and power and will, overbearing will, informing the whole personality.

A medal cast in commemoration of the ceremony showed Catherine seated; her head resting on her raised left arm and hand, while two male figures attired after the Roman fashion, one kneeling, are offering her the imperial crown placed on a cushion. For, however brought to the throne, the ruler of Russia received the crown that he or she might place it on his or her own head.

After the coronation came for the people the usual galas and entertainments which stretched, not over days, but over weeks. They were fully described with gusto by the Princess Daschkov in her memoirs; that young lady being as triumphant as ever Walpole had pictured her. But as the celebrations died down the trouble that had been foreseen made its appearance, more of it than was ever officially admitted.

On the whole, mildness had been the keynote of the treatment of those who had supported Peter. The Chancellor Vorontsov had been sent to live outside Russia; other officials had been expected to withdraw into private life. Nothing worse had happened to Elizabeth Vorontsov than to be ordered to return to her parents' house in Moscow, and not to show her face at court again. Catherine still pursued the rule that had been hers when treading her thorny path as Grand-duchess: to conciliate and win over any who might become dangerous enemies. Members of the families of both Shuvalov and Vorontsov continued to serve the Empress and the state.

The refusal to indulge in vindictive action was well advised and probably the vast majority of those around Catherine were of the opinion that Russia was well rid of Peter. Yet there were still many who resented the passing over of Peter's son in the succession to his father's throne. The appearance of the little Grand-duke at his mother's coronation had been the signal for a burst of shouting and cheering which in its excess might have been held to be somewhat ominous. There were, too, the inevitable discontents and jealousies, always fostered by a coup d'état.

Three outbreaks assumed a serious aspect. The first, which took place shortly after the coronation, originated in the army. In the second, which occurred in the following year, the standard of revolt was raised by an able and truculent ecclesiastic, the Archbishop of Rostov, it being understood that while the Empress proclaimed herself a devout daughter of the church— she never made the mistake, as Peter had done, of

87

belittling its ceremonies or of under-rating its influence—she intended to continue the policy of secularization of the church lands. Both revolts were quelled. The Archbishop was degraded and transferred, as simple monk, to a distant cloister. But in his diatribes against Catherine he had proclaimed, although for him it was a secondary matter, that the true heir to the throne was either the Grand-duke Paul or Ivan VI. Catherine should have been regent for the one, or might, in his opinion, have married the other. Then, within a year, the third and most violent outbreak did centre around the pitiful figure of the prisoner in the island fortress. A widespread political conspiracy aimed at getting rid of Catherine, rescuing the twenty-four-year-old Ivan, and placing him on the throne. Ivan paid with his life for the attempt to use him as a cat's-paw. He was strangled by his gaolers as the attack on the fortress was being made. Brückner, examining the evidence, has pronounced Catherine guiltless of the murder; but has pointed out that her undisguised relief at the news of the death, even as she deplored it, made an unfavourable impression on foreign diplomats. That manifestation of relief, no less than her earlier agitation, both evident, were witnesses to the stress to which the tidings of the conspiracy as they reached her had subjected her. The awareness of further danger, of the threat which the person of her own son offered to her security, never left her. It was a state of affairs that pulled the relationship between the two still further awry. Nor was the plot which had brought about the murder of Ivan by any means the last political intrigue Catherine had to face. Nevertheless, such as did occur came the more seldom to the surface as the Empress strengthened her position. Much had already been done; many foundations had already been laid, despite the disturbances, in the two years which had elapsed since the coronation.

During those years, and especially when conspiracies had threatened, Catherine had had steady support from Gregori Orlov and his following. On the coronation he had been given the title of Count, and a lavish grant of lands. Both within Russia and without, the possibility of a marriage between him and Catherine had been freely discussed. There was no marriage. Catherine went her way alone. Orlov presently ceased to be her lover and was replaced by another. But he remained at her side. It was not he, however, who became her chief minister. That position was given to Count Nikita Panin.

Some years since, Catherine and Sir Charles Hanbury-Williams had agreed that when the time came—the time to which both had steadily looked forward—Panin would make an excellent minister. In particular his diplomatic experience—he had been at Stockholm before going to Copenhagen— fitted him for a post in which his principal function would be to deal with foreign affairs.

To Catherine he had proved his worth in the events of the last years of Elizabeth; and in the happenings which had led up to her own succession, even though she knew that Panin had been among those who had planned for her a regency, not the crown. Working with Panin at first was Bestúzhev, brought back from exile, given a seat on the council and a pension. But Bestúzhev was an old and worn-out man and soon dropped out of the picture.

In the field of foreign policy one immediate decision had to be taken. The obsession of the late Emperor for Frederick and the terms of the agreement made with that prince had been one of the factors, perhaps the principal factor, which had brought about his own destruction. His widow and successor had to make up her mind, and to make it up quickly, what action Russia should take in relation to the war which had now been raging for six years. Maria Theresa and her ministers hoped for a complete reversal of policy; Russia acting with Austria against Prussia. Frederick had cause for the state of perturbation into which he found himself plunged at the news of the dethronement of his supporter, his disciple. Whatever his opinion on the subsequent murder it was not for him to be hampered by any scruples. Directly he learned of the proclamation of Catherine as Empress, he sent off a letter of warm congratulation and hopes and wishes for the future. Subsequent letters to St. Petersburg, following rapidly one after another, dwelt upon reasons why the terms of the treaty should be adhered to; and the understanding between Russia and Prussia continue. Catherine, with Panin acquiescing, took a middle course. She withdrew from all active participation in the war. It was made clear to Maria Theresa that Austria in her struggle against Prussia could look for no help from Russia. But simultaneously the Russian troops which Peter had sent to join Frederick's forces were withdrawn. The decision was a reflection of a principle that Catherine, while still Grand-duchess, had laid down and inscribed in her diary. She had written then that Russia, that great country, needed peace; and further, that peace would serve Russia's turn and ensure her a balance of power better than could war, which was always ruinous. As future events would show, this was far from ruling out for Catherine the possibility that to go to war might be necessary and even desirable. At this moment she judged it to be neither.

In the meantime England, regardless of Frederick's complaints that she was deserting him, was likewise withdrawing from the continental fighting in which she had neither been particularly interested, nor particularly successful. She was about to negotiate with France the terms, finally embodied in the Treaty of Paris, which marked her triumph as a naval and colonial power. But to Frederick, whatever his annoyance, the withdrawal of the

Russian and English troops counted for little in comparison with the fact that Maria Theresa was now facing him alone; for France could do nothing for her. And to Maria Theresa came the realization that any further attempt to regain Silesia was useless. On 15 February, 1763, five days after the signing of the Treaty of Paris, a treaty was signed at the hunting lodge by St. Hubertusberg in Saxony, which left the geographical position as it was at the beginning of the war. Frederick kept Silesia. He did not gain Saxony, which he had passionately desired and for which he had been prepared to give up East Prussia. He had his way, however, in his refusal to pay a penny of compensation to Saxony for the wrong done to her in his ruthless invasion. He also refused to allow Russia to participate in the negotiations for the peace that was to conclude a war from which she had withdrawn. So much revenge he accorded himself.

But the King of Prussia had no intention of quarrelling with the Empress of Russia. All his further observations confirmed, and strengthened, the high opinion he had formed of Catherine's ability. And she, on her side, had not lacked intelligence concerning Frederick of Prussia. The two, the woman of thirty-six and the man of fifty-one, understood each other very well; and no less well did they understand how the aims of both might be furthered by their co-operation. During 1764 began the correspondence between the two monarchs, which continued until the death of Frederick, and ultimately filled substantial volumes in the collections of letters in St. Petersburg and at Berlin. The pair discoursed to each other of many matters; paid each other compliments, couched in the elegant artificial style of the century. Likewise both were realists; and, as such, were aware that sooner, rather than later, questions vital to the relationship between their respective countries must arise.

Before this correspondence began, Catherine had been already absorbed in another. In 1762, François Marie Arouet Voltaire, the literary patriarch of Europe, was in his sixty-ninth year. For the past five years he had been living at Ferney, the estate on the French side of the French-Swiss frontier, four miles from Geneva, to which he had retired as a spot whence he could more safely carry on his fight against what he saw as the tyranny of church and state. He had long since taken an interest in Russia and was, indeed, just now completing his history of Peter the Great. This history had been undertaken at the request of Elizabeth, on the advice of Ivan Shuvalov, a nephew of Peter and Alexander. The latter, but especially Peter, had been, amid political activities, enthusiastic for learning. Their nephew was even more so.

Having thus given up his time to a study of Peter the Great, even while he had been observing what was going on in Russia, it was in the natural course of events that Voltaire's interest should

93

have been roused by the account he received of Catherine. The time was ripe for him to add yet another crowned head to his other royal correspondents. The ground had been no less well prepared on the side of Catherine. Reading Voltaire during the years past, absorbing his teaching, he had already become to her the master, at whose feet she was prepared to sit. An instrument of liaison between the two was ready to hand. One of Catherine's secretaries, Picton, was a native of Geneva; and a disciple of this historian-philosopher who had taken up his abode on the shores of the lake. When all Europe had been buzzing with stories as to what had happened at Oranienbaum, in St. Petersburg and at Ropsha, Picton had sent a long despatch to Ferney. Its contents had been designed to explain to Voltaire the nature of the intolerable position in which Catherine had found herself, forcing her to take action against her husband. Catherine must, in short, be vindicated in the eyes of Voltaire. And vindicated she had been. Within the next few months Empress and philosopher plunged into an exchange of letters which were to continue to pass to and fro between them until the end of Voltaire's life. Neither this correspondence nor that with Frederick the Great was unique. In a letter-writing age Catherine was a prolific letter-writer. And if her style did not place her in the rank of a Madame de Sévigné, the letters are an admirable expression of what she observed and of

94

her ideas. Each section of her correspondence has its significance. That with Voltaire, added to that conducted with his fellow-philosophers—the letters to Grimm are often said to be the best example of Catherine's thought and her epistolary style—has been seen, especially in conjunction with her reading, as of particular importance.

Catherine was a natural autocrat—of that there was never any doubt—and at the back of her autocracy, fortifying it, lay her interpretation of philosophic ideas and ideals. In this she was not unique. The age of reason, the age of rulers instructed by the philosophers, nourished the autocrat-ruler who was described as benevolent or enlightened. Such rulers, and among them Catherine was conspicuous, had no doubt but that their will must be supreme; and they were the more autocrats, because of their conviction that this will was guided by the right principles. The natural corollary was the demand, conscious or unconscious, that others should recognize how wise, how beneficial, how intrinsically good, were the foundations of their rule, the decisions they took. Herein Catherine received ample support from such letters as those of Voltaire and Grimm. She had, moreover, attained the throne of a country, the theory and structure of whose government offered peculiar scope for the exercise of benevolent despotism.

The position of the crown in Russia in relation to the nation at large assumed and provided for the wielding of absolute power by a ruler who was regarded as the head of a family. The title of Little Father, as applied to that ruler, had a real meaning. But the Little Father was likewise, as Peter had emphasized in his adoption of the imperial title, the emperor-autocrat. The form that the government had assumed meant that the country was administered by a body of men responsible to the crown alone.

Closest to the sovereign, since at least the days of Peter the Great, was a small shifting body of ministers of no recognized status or composition, and called into being solely by the will of the sovereign. In the course of her reign Catherine contemplated creating out of this body a permanent Council of State. But although steps were taken to that end, it was not fully accomplished in her time. As had been the practice of her predecessors, she also made considerable use of commissions summoned for particular purposes.

The permanent and principal instrument of government was the senate, established by Peter the Great. Its members had been from the first the nominees of the crown, and owed no responsibility elsewhere. Their original number had been nine, with a small secretariat. But even in the time of the founder, that number had been augmented. After his death there had been steady expansion of both senate and secretariat. With certain alterations, among which were a number made by Catherine, the senate continued to function until imperial Russia itself disappeared, controlling the administration, both central and provincial, as well as the judiciary.

Up to the accession of Peter the Great the administrative business of the country had been carried on by a number of departments, originating from many different sources. These departments had been reconstructed by Peter on the collegiate principle. Eight colleges were named at first, with an additional three later; each having as its head a small board or council; and all designed to work one with another. That hope was disappointed. By the time that Catherine took up Peter's sceptre, the collegiate principle was very largely a thing of the past. Three of the so-called colleges, that of the army; of the navy; and of foreign affairs, were well on the way to become three independent ministries; a process that was completed under Catherine.

Lastly, for the purposes of local administration, Peter had divided Russia into eight provinces, each with its own governor and each again subdivided.

Peter had, as he thought, provided for the functioning of the various administrative bodies by the decrees which exacted universal service. And, even when this conception was, in 1762, finally shattered, a very large number of the upper classes did, as a matter of course, remain in the civil administration, even as in the army and in

97

the navy. Nor, as before, was any insuperable barrier imposed to the advancement of anyone, whatever his social status and at whatever level he had begun. A further characteristic was the number of foreigners to be found in the administrative, the naval and the military services. These men came from all over Europe, not excluding the British Isles; often invited and always encouraged by Peter and his successors. So coming, many of them remained and in a number of cases received, as the father of Nikita Panin had done, a Russian title.

The machinery with which the government thus outlined worked, both at the centre and in the provincial districts, was, despite the efforts at simplification made by Peter the Great, slow, awkward and complex; dependent upon customs rooted in the past, differing one from another according to where they were found; and upon a mass of laws which was not inaccurately described by a contemporary ambassador as a perfect chaos. Not infrequently the sovereign, in whom the legislative power alone rested, or a minister to whom that power was delegated, had issued a law which contradicted one of an earlier date without the latter being annulled.

The more enlightened officials had long since seen the necessity for reducing the confusion to some sort of order. In this view Catherine completely concurred. She saw, too, as others had seen, that the remedy should be the drawing up of a new code. The idea that thus presented itself was peculiarly agreeable to her.

The first step was to summon an assembly whose duty should be to consider what was required; and, it was hoped, what might be done. Before that assembly was called Catherine determined to provide the members for their guidance with a set of rules which should embody the principles upon which, in her view, at least, laws should be founded.

Upon this document, which was subsequently known, from the purpose for which it was intended, as the *Instructions*, she worked for nearly two years. For her the exercise, linked up with her past reading and thought, must have been pleasurable; all her references to the work convey as much. No less pleasurable must have been the discussions which she permitted and even encouraged to take place with those to whom she chose to communicate the results of her labours. The exchange of ideas, whether in writing or in speech, was a feature of the age; and Catherine was not the least eager of its exponents. Nor were the discussions purely academic. Catherine accepted many emendations and alterations. Much of what she had first put down was, she wrote to D'Alembert, torn up or burnt. The whole, as it finally appeared, was, she told him, a compromise. That compromise was between Catherine's theories and the opinions of those who saw in the practical application of the theories the complete upheaval of the social system they knew.

The ideas which Catherine set down were, as she herself again said, derived from her past reading. When the document was made public, no student of political thought could fail to perceive that the greater part thereof was taken either from Montesquieu's *Spirit of the Laws*, the book Catherine had so eagerly read in the days when her vigorous, active mind had found its outlet in reading; or from Beccaria's book entitled *Crime and Punishment*, which had appeared in 1764. Something had been added by Catherine herself. And there were modifications advised by others.

The general line of thought was illustrated by the opening pronouncements: that the Christian law teaches people to do good one to another as much as possibly can be done; that every honest man in the community will wish to see his country happy, glorious, safe and tranquil; and himself to live under a law which protects, but does not oppress. In the sections dealing with that law it is laid down that only what is prejudicial to either the community or the individual should be forbidden; that all should be equal in the sight of the law; that all must obey the law; but also that all must be free to do all that the law does not forbid.

And so with crime and punishment. More consideration should be given to the prevention of crime than to the infliction of punishment. Careful distinction should be drawn between crimes of different natures, and differing in significance. Capital punishment should be resorted to as seldom as might be. Torture should be completely prohibited.

In these and in such sections as those dealing with police and justice can be observed the influence of the humanitarian school of thought, the school whose ideal was the freedom of the individual within an ordered society; the school which accepted the view of Locke that law and freedom were necessary to one another, since the one could not exist without the other. It was the school to which Catherine would have claimed, and in some respects would have been justified in claiming, that she gave her allegiance. Nevertheless, in the document appeared two features which in reality vitiated all the principles thus set forth.

The first of these was the doctrine of the absolutism of the crown. So far from retreating from this doctrine, Catherine emphasized it. Unequivocally it was stated that the sovereign is supreme; is the sole source of all civil and political power; is subject to no check. True, the sovereign is there to serve the people. But that service is seen to be solely dependent on his or her will to good. Diderot, reading the document, summed up the position; the Empress of Russia, he wrote, is certainly a despot, since, whatever the true end of her government, it makes all liberty and property depend on one person.

For the other contradictory feature Catherine

was not herself entirely responsible. It lay in the treatment of serfdom. On the evidence available, there is something to be said for believing that Catherine was quite sincere in the views which, in the early years, she expressed on the subject. Her study of philosophy had taught her that serfdom was an affront to the individual. Her own acumen helped her to see it also as a festering sore, which sooner or later would poison the whole community. A reflection of these views, by no means in an extreme form, appeared in her original draft, and about the time when that draft was being drawn up she founded a society known as the Imperial Free Economic Society, one of whose objects was to be discussion of the problem of the peasant. But it was just here that Catherine had to capitulate. Even an absolute sovereign, and Catherine was no exception, rather the contrary, cannot entirely disregard the views of those upon whom he or she must rely to keep him or her in power; those who are necessary to maintain what in the *Instructions* was termed the safety of the institution of monarchy. In the opinion of many of those whom Catherine consulted, her approach to the alleviation, if not the abolition of serfdom, struck at the very foundations of society; as at the economic welfare of the country. They protested. As a result, in their final form, the *Instructions* committed themselves only to the general statements that serfdom should exist only in the interests of the state; that it ought to be a rare condition; that it would, however, be extremely dangerous to free all serfs at once. The Free Economic Society itself, having offered a prize for an essay on the condition of the peasant, forbade the publication of that of the winner, since he had advocated peasant proprietors.

The *Instructions* were drawn up for a specific purpose in the Russian language for Russia. But cognizance of them was taken outside Russia; translations were made, and the interest excited was considerable. In ministerial circles in England, according to the correspondence with the embassy in St. Petersburg, there was something of a tendency to treat the whole as an example of rhetorical theory which would not have, and, according to some, was not intended to have, any practical results. Some hasty judgment was based on a lack of comprehension that what Catherine had in mind bore no relation to the English parliamentary system, and had but little indeed in common with the English constitution as a whole. In France the document, or rather what might come of it, was viewed much more seriously. So dangerous did the authorities find the liberal views expressed therein that publication was strictly forbidden. But Catherine had her full meed of praise from others. Among them, Frederick of Prussia, to whom she had sent a translation in German made especially for him, overwhelmed her with flattery, and made her a member of the Berlin Academy. With Voltaire there had been correspondence during the making of the *Instructions*. It was not until the December of 1768 that Catherine was able to despatch to Ferney a complete version in French, written, not printed, since, as she explained, there had been no time to get this done. She received a more than favourable verdict. Lycurgus and Solon, wrote the philosopher, might have put their name to the work; they could not have composed it.

The date appended to the *Instructions* was 30 July (10 August, N.S.), 1767. This was the day for the first meeting of the assembly for whose benefit they had been prepared.

That assembly consisted, according to one set of official figures, of five hundred and sixty-four members; and those members were drawn from a very wide field. It was, in fact, intended that they should represent all the classes who made up the people of Russia; and to a very large extent they did so. The total number was made up of two hundred and eight representatives of the towns; one hundred and sixty-one of the nobility; and seventy-four of the peasants, with twenty-eight of government officials. The remaining eighty-eight were drawn from the Cossack communities, and from those outlying districts referred to as foreign, since their inhabitants were not, strictly speaking, racially Russian. Only the clergy, who had their own synod, with which Peter the Great had replaced their ancient patriarchate, had, as a body, no representative. A number, however, were present in the assembly in various capacities. In the gathering as a whole, the figure given for the official delegates may well have been doubled by the presence of other persons of all ranks in a variety of capacities.

All these members were in theory to have been chosen by the communities whom they were to represent; and in practice this had been done to a certain extent. It was probably inevitable that in many cases those who had to choose were bewildered as to what was this new thing that was required of them. On the whole, opinion saw in the gathering a fairly accurate cross-section of the Russian people.

The place of assembly was the Kremlin; and there the members continued to meet until the beginning of the next year, when they moved to St. Petersburg. The president was the Marshal Bibikov, a prominent soldier and statesman. He had been nominated by Catherine; and she herself was almost continuously in Moscow during the months when the Assembly was sitting there. Gregori Orlov, who had been one of those to whom the early drafts of the *Instructions* had been shown, and who had approved them, was one of the elected members, and appears to have played a prominent part throughout. Of those closest to Catherine, he probably held the most Slavophil opinions, and it seems certain that he was also one of the more enlightened of the nobility in his desire for an improvement in the conditions of serfdom, and possibly even for its abolition.

The discussions of the Assembly were based on the mandates, or reports which each group had been required to bring with them. It was intended that these reports should set forth the needs of each particular class represented; and, as such, they afforded a valuable, if not comprehensive, picture of social conditions. In that picture two subjects were in the foreground. Of these the one, as already foreshadowed in the discussions on the preliminary draft, was precisely the key question of serfdom. In the Assembly the fundamental cleavage of opinion was apparent. There appeared to be no bridge which could span the gulf between those who said that serfdom must continue, some out of self-interest pure and simple, but some because they held it to be absolutely necessary in the interests of agriculture and of the country at large; and the others, those who represented the peasants, together with the more enlightened and humanitarian members, who spoke of the evils of serfdom and the human misery engendered by the condition.

The second subject which forced its way to the front was that of the relation between the central and local administration. Much of the

discussion was devoted to the conflicting claims
of the two authorities, with no definite conclusion
reached. Nevertheless, it was in the field of
provincial government that the most serious, if
not the only serious attempt at reorganization
was to be made. By a series of edicts, including
further and extensive divisions of the country as
begun by Peter; new appointments of governors
and other officials; and the establishment of new
courts, including courts of justice, something was
accomplished in the way of systematizing what
had hitherto, in spite of Peter the Great,
remained inchoate and largely inefficient. Yet
the success was only partial; and the new order
placed ultimately more and more power in the
hands of the landowners, on whom the crown
had to depend for its working.

Another debate in the Assembly revealed a
further gulf between two sections of society.
Long since, Peter the Great had seen the
importance for Russia of trade, both at home
and abroad, and hence the importance of the
merchant class. Catherine once more followed
his lead. One of the not least interesting sections
of her *Instructions* had dealt with the question of
the merchants. When, however, the latter
presented their report to the Assembly, what
ensued was very largely a wrangle between them
and the landowners. The merchants charged the
latter with selfish consideration for their own
interests alone; whereby they abducted or

persuaded labour away from the towns, and ate up the resources of the state. To that the land-owners retorted that it was the merchants who lived a purely self-centred existence, in that they pursued trade for their own benefit, rather than for the benefit of the state, adding that they had certainly never fulfilled the hopes of Peter the Great. So again the arguments, as set forth, brought no concrete result.

Save only for the partial and, to some extent, dubious reforms in provincial administration, the same was true of the Assembly as a whole. No new code, nor even an approach to a new code, emerged from its labours. Even if the problem of the government of Russia had not been so vast a one, like the country itself, there had been no real preparation for an expedient that held so much that was so new and so strange. The true importance of the Assembly derived from the fact that it was ever called at all; and even more from the drawing up and the presentation of the mandates, although some of these had not been read when the meeting, after some eighteen months, broke up, and the members returned to their homes.

Chapter Five

Russia and Poland

THE closing of the commission which it had
been hoped would have laid the foundations
for a new legislative code for Russia coincided
with the intensification of another phase in
Catherine's career as a ruler—Catherine was of
those of whom it may be said that to wear a
crown was to have a career. As she said of herself, her métier was to govern. The vision that it
might be her function to reform the government
of Russia never completely faded. But it grew
dim and was relegated to the background as
other projects claimed her attention, and, of
these, that to which she had now turned was to
absorb the greater part of her energies to the
end of her life. It was that of the frontiers of
Russia; thought of in terms in which the aim of
security on the one hand was closely intertwined
with that of expansion on the other. Her energy,
her political acumen, her grandiose imagination,
carried her forward on a path already in part
trodden out by those who had gone before her.

The Mongol invasions of the thirteenth century
had left only a core of Muscovite land, surrounding the city of Moscow, whose princes made

their city the capital, as Kiev had been the capital of the earlier Russia.

From the fifteenth century onwards had come the slow pushing out from this core, here a thick wedge and there a narrow tongue, to the north and to the south, to the east and to the west. And each of these forward movements, while it strengthened the country that was to be the new great Russia, had brought its own peculiar problems. Each movement, too, had its own characteristics. That to the west in particular had differed markedly in one respect from all the others. Elsewhere the thrust had been in the main directed against nomad peoples beyond whom, to the east and to the south, lay another continent, another civilization, Asia and her peoples. But the frontier line of the west, from the Baltic almost to the Black Sea, where the nomadic began again, was that of organized states.

There, with their Baltic coastline were Livonia and Esthonia; and, beyond them, the Duchy of Courland, also with its long Baltic shore. Beyond the Duchy again, with more Baltic coastline, a coastline which was broken up by the Brandenburg possession, known as East Prussia, was the kingdom of Poland; stretching southward to the river Dniester and the Carpathians. And, there, southwards once more, lay the Balkan peninsula, the territory of the Turks in Europe.

Already, before Catherine's day, there had

been an advance along the Baltic shore. Even before Peter the Great had opened his window to the west, the rulers of sixteenth-century Muscovy had perceived the need, if they were to carry on a successful trade, of free access to that sea. True, after Richard Chancellor had made his memorable voyage, the White Sea route, with its port at Archangel, had been developed. But it was a dangerous, difficult and long route in comparison with that by way of the Baltic, and was, too, ice-bound for a much longer period of the year. Hence, the constant attempts to push through to the Baltic coast, until Peter, having overcome Sweden with her claims to supremacy in that sea, and having forced his way to those shores, gained by treaty Livonia and Esthonia, with their harbours of Revel and Riga. There remained the Duchy of Courland. That country had long owed allegiance to Poland. It continued to do so. But with the absorption of its two neighbours, the Duchy itself became ever more subject to Russian influence.

As part of his western policy, Peter had encouraged the immigration of Germans into all three of the Baltic countries. Known as Baltic Germans, many of these settlers began to play an important part in the countries of their adoption; and, in the days of the Empress Anne, one of them, Biron, became ruler of the Duchy of Courland. He proved an unpopular ruler, and was ultimately removed and sent to Siberia.

Then, in 1758, with Elizabeth on the throne of Russia, four years from the end of her reign, a request reached the Russian court. The King of Poland at the time was Augustus III, who was also Elector of Saxony. Augustus now requested the Empress Elizabeth of Russia to sanction the succession of his son, Charles, to the Dukedom of Courland. Elizabeth had seen no objection and had consented. Among many who disagreed with her had been the Grand-duchess Catherine. But her opinion carried no weight with the Empress. The young man was installed as Duke of Courland.

So matters had stood when Catherine became Empress. Then, in 1763, she had acted. Determined that this royal house of Saxony in Poland should not obtain hereditary rights in Courland, through the person of the young man who was now duke, she proceeded to get him out. Her appeal was to the Polish Diet, as usual at loggerheads with their elected king. To the Diet, she pointed out that their rights were threatened by their monarch, a foreigner, having obtained an hereditary dukedom for his son. Those rights, she declared, she was ready to defend. She had gone on to reinforce these arguments by herself providing a ruler for Courland. Biron was recalled from Siberia and ordered to take over the Duchy, a scheme which was supported by the sending thither of Russian troops. In April 1763, Charles of Saxony left Courland. The incident, for this in relation to future events it was, ended thus in triumph for Catherine. The whole occurrence was the logical outcome of the frontier policy of Peter the Great. It also proved to be the logical beginning of that of Catherine. She turned, the same year, to Poland itself; and with Poland the Grand-duchy of Lithuania, united to the former country in a kind of federal union. The history of this Duchy contained the seeds of much of the trouble.

When a century after their occupation of the greater part of the country that was afterwards to be United Russia, the power of the Mongols had begun to weaken, other invading forces under a series of remarkable leaders had appeared on the Dnieper and in the district between that river and the Dniester. They had come from Lithuania, the narrow strip of country by the Baltic, a country whose people in the fourteenth century were still heathen. They had come, they had conquered, they had fought the Mongols, they had fought the Russians; they had taken Kiev and had created the great fortress town of Brest-Litovsk. Twenty years and more before the fourteenth century had run out, Lithuanian rule had extended from the Baltic to the Black Sea; and in 1386 had come the event of significance, even of portent, for the future. In that year, Jagellon, Duke of Lithuania, had married Hedwig, heiress to the Polish throne; and, perhaps as the price of that marriage, he and his people had accepted Christianity, and were baptized in the Roman communion. Henceforth Poland and Lithuania, together forming a great kingdom to the west of Russia, had been united, first by a dynasty in common, and after 1569 in a kind of federal union. Had matters gone otherwise, had Lithuania looked east and not west, had her ruler accepted the Orthodox form of Christianity instead of the Roman; had there come about, as well might have been the case, union not with Poland, but with Russia, the course of history might have run differently.

Always Russia had resented the creation of this kingdom of Lithuania-Poland. There was the offence to the sense of history. To whatever power and dignity first Moscow, and then St. Petersburg had risen, Kiev had been the mother city of Russia, the soil from which Russia had sprung. Next, the kingdom, with its western associations, was seen as a political menace to Russia. Lastly, there were the questions of race and religion. There continued in Lithuania many Russians, in the main those known as White Russians, one of the many races of which Russia was ethnologically made up. They were, and remained, distinct from the Lithuanians, who had swept in from the north. Here, too, was a dividing line in religion. The Russian dwellers in Lithuania were either adherents of the Orthodox Church, or had become Uniats, members of the church which at the end of the sixteenth century had evolved a sort of halfway house between the Orthodox and the Roman communions.

On every ground seeds of trouble had thus, from the first, existed as between Russia and Lithuania-Poland. They had come to fruition.

The federal union of 1569 had been the work of a congress held at Lublin. This congress had done two other things. It had made the crown of Poland elective. It had given Poland increased authority over Kiev and the Dniester lands. It marked the climax of Poland's great period under the house of Jagellon. It was also a pointer to the beginning of the end.

During the following century, Poland, under elected kings—the house of Jagellon became extinct—had suffered pressure on all sides, and in spite of some brilliant interludes had grown ever weaker. Her geographical alignment, the spreading plains with no effective barriers between her and her neighbours, rendered her vulnerable. Gradually Russia had begun to advance into Lithuania, until in 1667 the rich prize of Kiev with the district known as Little Russia had been ceded by truce to Russia, a truce confirmed twenty-two years later.

There had followed more or less peace, with a frontier more or less stable, until, in 1763, Catherine had begun a series of new moves.

In spite of the recovery by Russia of a great part of Lithuania, that which remained of the kingdom of Lithuania-Poland was still looked on by Russia as a hindrance, if not a danger, to the growth of the Russian state. Poland, on its side, as represented by its aristocracy, its landed gentry and its church, thought in terms of the defence of western culture and of catholicism against the approach of another civilisation; another church. Since the magnates, acting with the church, controlled both the legislature and the executive—later one single member of the Diet could veto any reform —they, in actuality if not in theory, controlled the crown also. As for the peasants, they, early in the seventeenth century, had been disfranchised and reduced to serfdom.

In making the crown elective the congress of Lublin had created a system which held many threatening features, not the least of which was that any foreign candidate, whether he were a crowned head or no, might be elected. Thus foreign intervention, on the demise of the crown, was not only possible but positively invited. And foreign candidates had from the first lost no time in making their appearance. When, in 1696, the Elector of Saxony had been elected as Augustus II, it had been from among eighteen candidates of many nationalities, each backed by foreign powers; and by parties within Poland itself. An endeavour by Polish patriots to elect a Pole as his successor on his death in 1733 had been frustrated by Austria and Russia. He had been succeeded after what can only be described as a bitterly fought election, by his son, who ruled as Augustus III.

The thirty years' reign of this monarch had been marked by the Courland incident. But on the whole, he had shown himself mild and easy-going, disinclined for any kind of conflict. His death, in the autumn of 1763, was, as it proved, to be more important than had been his life. Catherine, to the east of Poland, Frederick to the west, had laid their plans. Each of the two saw those plans as the more urgent because the death of the Polish king coincided with the emergence in Poland of a strong national movement.

Amid all the chances and changes which had befallen the crown and the country, Poland had always retained a fundamental national feeling. No less had she thrown up at intervals men of outstanding character and ability. It had long been her tragedy and was now, that such leaders remained brilliant individuals, unable to weld together a state divided among itself, even in the periods when ideas of reform came to the fore.

A strong party among the magnates was at the moment acutely aware of the dangers to which the system of election to the crown exposed the country. They brought forward a plan to abolish the elective kingship and to replace it by an hereditary dynasty. Under this scheme Charles, son of the late king, was to succeed his father, and, as that father had planned long since, was to

117

become Duke of Courland also; driving out Biron and the Russians.

There was to be likewise a reform of the legislature and executive.

The plans were good, even admirable, as far as they went. Only too soon they were seen to have their foundations on sand. On the one hand there was soon evident what appeared to be fundamental differences of opinion amounting to antagonism towards each other among the various groups within the country itself. At the same time, beyond the frontiers, neither Catherine nor Frederick had any intention of permitting the development of a strong, independent Poland. The correspondence between the two sovereigns, no less than the political testament drawn up by Frederick, which appeared after his death, leaves little doubt what was in the mind of each.

Catherine, at all events, at first appears to have visualized a Poland which should retain its entity, as it was after the incorporation, a century earlier, of the main part of Lithuania-Poland which historically and racially could be claimed as Russian. But it was to be a Poland subject to the guidance and influence of Russia; in short, dominated by that country. Here Catherine parted company with Nikita Panin.

That minister's policy was influenced by his desire to create a system of northern alliances and so strengthen the position of Russia in the Baltic. It was an idea that to some extent derived from his earlier diplomatic connection with Denmark; and with Sweden; with the latter country in particular. His scheme would have included proposed subsidies for Sweden at least. Intent upon this plan he personally would not have objected to a strong, independent and reformed Poland, who would be willing to act in alliance with Russia.

The attitude of Frederick was, on the other hand, from the first, predatory. He desired to annex the western part of Poland in order to round off his kingdom, even as he had desired Silesia which he had gained, and Saxony which he had not.

Under these circumstances, both sovereigns were well aware how delicate was the situation between them, how easily it might become critical. But two astute minds understood each other very well. This was to be no occasion for war, nor even for an acute diplomatic crisis. Presently affairs were put into train.

At first sight, the early moves of the political game, with Poland as the pawn, appeared to give the advantage to Catherine. She had a candidate for the vacant throne in Stanislas Poniatowski, the young Polish nobleman who nine years before had come to St. Petersburg in the train of Sir Charles Hanbury-Williams; and had replaced Sergei Saltikov as Catherine's lover. He, in his turn, had had to give place to Gregori Orlov. But he had never been lost sight of and now Catherine had a part ready for him to play. Here, she pointed out to Frederick, was a suitable king for Poland. And Frederick, biding his time, acquiesced. In April 1764, six months after the death of Augustus, a compact was signed between Catherine and Frederick whereby the two agreed to bring pressure to bear on the Polish Diet in favour of Stanislas.

In many respects the young man was not an unacceptable candidate. His father's family, if not particularly distinguished, could claim long descent and some royal connections. More important, his mother had been a Czartoryski, a member of the family which, by tradition strongly inclined to Russia in their sympathies, played a powerful part in Polish politics. In his person, too, the young man had much to recommend him. To the good looks and the charm which, those years since in St. Petersburg, the Grand-duchess had been quick to perceive, were added a vivid intelligence and an appreciation of art and literature. He had been a conspicuous figure on a prolonged visit to England, where he had taken much interest in the English political system. He was equally well known in Paris. But amid all his graces those who knew him were well aware of a fatal defect. He lacked strength of character and purpose.

On 7 September—according to the western dating—1764, Stanislas was formally elected King of Poland. Catherine wrote a self-congratulatory letter to Panin, in which she referred to the king which they had made. She might have added, what she knew perfectly well, that this was the king whom she would be able to direct; and, no less might she have pointed out that the king had been made without the interference that might, under different conditions, have been expected. In particular Austria and France had both been observing Catherine and Frederick with suspicion. But, exhausted by the Seven Years War, neither was ready to oppose the election, nor to take any action whatsoever.

As had so often been the case the discord prevailing among the Polish magnates and the landed gentry had weakened their power to act effectively. That weakness had given Catherine, and Frederick acting with her, the opportunity to put in their puppet king, admirably suited for the part he was required to play. In Catherine's view this part would be played by the acceptance of direction from St. Petersburg. What was in Frederick's mind was apparent later.

The ground was prepared for direction from St. Petersburg by the presence in Warsaw, as Russian representative, of Prince Anakita Rapnin, nephew to Nikita Panin. The latter had as collaborators that section of Polish officials who were prepared to act with Russia. As backing he and they had Russian gold and Russian troops. The king, now known as Stanislas Augustus, for one, sorely needed that Russian gold, since he was always in debt. His supporters knew, even if he did not, that at any moment Russian troops might be necessary if he were to remain on the throne.

But the subordination to Russia was not really complete. Almost immediately disaffection, not confined to any one group, began to raise its head. It was to be found among those more enlightened nobles and magnates who had been planning reforms. There were also those who, whether belonging to the former group or not, were exponents of a passionate nationalism which bitterly resented all direction from Russia; lastly, the Church of Rome had to be reckoned with.

That church had the allegiance of the majority of the population of Poland. There remained, in what was left of Lithuania and elsewhere, a certain number of communities whose members professed the Orthodox faith, while in the west Lutheranism was a strong influence. Originally both Orthodox and Lutheran congregations had enjoyed a considerable measure of freedom of worship. As, however, the movement of the counter-reformation grew in strength so did the zeal and power of the Church of Rome within Poland prove too much for the dissenting groups. The toleration extended to them was gradually whittled down until by the time Stanislas ascended the throne it might be said to have completely disappeared; and something very like persecution to have begun.

From the point of view of Rome the situation justified drastic measures. Ecclesiastical authority saw itself threatened everywhere by the teaching and influence of the encyclopædists and philosophers. Both Frederick and Catherine, one on either side of Poland, were disciples of Voltaire. They were more than this. The one was the head of a Lutheran state. The other ruled a country of huge territories and teeming population whose church was not of the West, but of the East. Rome saw clearly the danger to its church and to Poland.

The keynote of Catherine's policy had been sounded as early as October, 1762, when, within a month of her coronation, she had impressed on the Russian envoy in Warsaw the necessity for the protection of all Poles professing the Orthodox faith. With the accession of her puppet king she was prepared to push matters further.

The advent of Stanislas had encouraged the Orthodox and Lutheran communities, commonly known as Dissendents, who had been working for the renewal of the right to worship, without interference, in their own buildings. But the representatives of the Roman communion, ecclesiastical and lay alike, stood firm. The hope of the Dissendents rested upon the possibility of support from without, in particular from Russia.

That Catherine would be ready to follow up the instructions sent to the Russian envoy in 1762 was a foregone conclusion. Her turn of mind, nourished on her reading, informed her, as she revealed in her comments on ecclesiastical ceremonies and customs, that there was much in all churches that was unacceptable to the philosophic spirit. The same line of thought gave her a genuine feeling for toleration, provided that did not threaten the political structure she believed to be beneficent for those over whom she had been called to rule. But, politically, first and foremost she had identified herself with the Orthodox Church into which she had been received as a girl of fifteen, even as she had identified herself with Russia. Frederick, who knew his Catherine, remarked of her that she had really no religion, but that she simulated devotion. The remark was very true. Catherine the realist saw clearly the importance of the part played by the Church in Russia, and no less clearly, the part it must play in the expansion of Russian influence.

Yet it was Frederick rather than Catherine who, in the case of Poland, was the first to bring matters to a head. That monarch was impatient for any development which would give him an opportunity to secure the lands upon which his gaze was fixed. Insistence upon the rights of the Lutherans within Poland—rights in which he probably quite genuinely believed, but the belief was cover for much else—was to him an obvious course of action.

Backed then both by Prussia and by Russia the Dissendents stated their case and put forward their demands. Stanislas Augustus, as ever in need of Russian gold and of Russian support in general, hesitated. The Diet, overwhelmingly Catholic, showed no such hesitation. Once more they stated there was to be no toleration. And the threat of conflict loomed ever more menacing. In 1767 the meeting of an extraordinary Diet called to consider the situation was marked by the highly inflammatory speeches of speakers who included among them Polish ecclesiastics as well as the Papal Nuncio. Catherine moved. Three of the most aggressive speakers, two of them bishops, were escorted to Russia. The following year another Diet was called and bullied by Rapnin into promising the Dissendents not only freedom of belief and worship, but of equal rights in every respect with members of the Church of Rome. The inevitable repercussions followed. In the years which had elapsed since the election of Stanislas Augustus the Catholic national and anti-Russian party had increased its membership and strengthened its influence. Nor had they, in their turn, been without encouragement from outside, particularly from France and Austria; on grounds of religion; and on grounds of politics since the rulers of both countries desired nothing more earnestly than to curb the growing and alarming power of both Russia and Prussia. For four years the opposition had smouldered. Now, in the spring of 1768, the conflagration burst forth.

The movement among the opposition party had largely taken the form of groups or confederations. The most formidable of these became known as the Confederation of Bar. The name derived from a meeting of representatives of the Catholic national party which had taken place at the little town of Bar or Barrow, near the Turkish frontier, between February and April. At that meeting they had declared the deposition of Stanislas Augustus; and had announced the formation of a national federation for which they invited national support. Within a few weeks civil war broke out. On the one side was the Confederation of Bar, with all those who had rallied to their cause; on the other were the intermingled groups, representing those who were prepared to stand by the king, as well as the more extreme who were ready to go to any length in support of Russia. This latter side had the advantage of support from a Russian force. That force shortly had, as its second-in-command, a soldier who was to go down in Russian history as one of their outstanding military leaders.

Alexander Suvorov had been destined for a civil career, mainly because his father had believed that his health was too poor to withstand the rigours of a soldier's life, but the boy, from his earliest days, had showed, to the surprise of his family, something which amounted to a passion for military history and military technique. The father had to consent to his entering the army. Under the regulations drawn up in the days of Peter the Great, he was forced to begin as a private, as he was over the age when it was permissible to join as an officer. It was more than six years later, in 1754, that he attained that rank. Serving as an officer, on the Prussian front, during the Seven Years War, he had added to the experience already gained by study and in practice as private and non-commissioned officer. When Russia had withdrawn from the war in 1762 he had been set to work at training. Now, in 1768, he reappeared in the field, to act against the Polish troops as brigadier and second-in-command.

Suvorov had the disadvantage of comparatively small forces against much more numerous forces of the confederation. He also had to act in what was to him a strange country, whereas it was familiar ground to his opponents. But in the fighting of the following two years, fighting that was in the nature of skirmishes rather than of pitched battles, he showed his quality as a commander, breaking up and smashing the groups in which the Poles were combating, whenever opportunity offered. It was, however, evident that the struggle would be a prolonged one. Before the end came the story of Poland was to become intermingled with, and in the end, disastrously affected by, that of her southern neighbour, Turkey.

Chapter Six

Russia and Turkey

A S the course of events in Poland had unfolded
both France and Austria had been watching
the progress of Catherine with no less alarm than
they had been watching that of Frederick. They
had had to acquiesce in the election of Catherine's
candidate to the Polish throne. Now, five years
later, both were somewhat recovered from their
war exhaustion; and France, in particular, under
the guidance of her able Foreign Minister,
Choiseul, thought the time had come to endeavour
to check the westward advance of Russia. A
method founded on tradition lay to hand.

An important factor in French foreign policy
had long been support of Turkey in Europe, a
weapon to be used against other powers when, and
if, necessary. In the past that weapon had been
employed mainly against Austria. Choiseul was
now persuaded that it could be turned against
Russia. His diplomatic activities to that end were
facilitated by the uneasiness amounting to alarm
with which the Sultan, Mustapha III, a man of
warlike disposition, and his advisers, had likewise
been watching the advance of Russia. Political
considerations loomed large, but the appeal for

opposition to Russia was founded on something more. It was an appeal to Islam against the Orthodox Church; bringing once more to the fore ancient enmities and ancient passions.

Three events, far back in the past, were links in a chain which, in the eighteenth century, was leading to other events of much import.

Nearly 800 years earlier, in 988, Vladimir, Prince of Kiev, had accepted Christianity. The church into which he and his people had been baptized had been the Greek, otherwise the Orthodox Church. Nearly five centuries later again, the tide of Ottoman invaders of Europe, who had succeeded the Mongol invaders, had swept up to the gates of Constantinople itself. The city had fallen; the last emperor had died fighting on the walls; St. Sofia had been transformed into a Moslem mosque. Another fourteen years had passed. There had come a marriage. The emperor had left, as his heiress, his niece Zoe Paleologus. After the catastrophe the girl had become a ward of the Pope. In 1472, that Pope's successor, Sixtus IV, had offered her hand to Ivan the Great believing that so might the Orthodox Church be reconciled to Rome; and the old schism closed. The result was exactly the contrary. On her marriage Zoe had been received into the Orthodox Church and had been re-baptized Sophia. Her husband had adopted the double-headed eagle of Byzantium as the royal crest and had become in his own eyes successor of the line of Paleologus, the natural champion of the church for which that line stood.

Apart from the question of the church, the capital of the Greek emperors, with all its splendour and colour, with its great tradition of art, had always been a magnet for the eager eyes of the princes of Kiev and after them those of the princes of Moscow. It was an attraction backed up by the material considerations of the trade, which, ever and anon interrupted by merciless warfare, had passed between Kiev and Constantinople; and over and beyond this, it was the latter city, which guarded the straits through which Russian ships must pass if they were to reach the Mediterranean and the world beyond.

At the same time the path of the Turks into Europe as they had followed their Mongol predecessors had created another and more immediate vital problem for Russia. That path had lain along the shores of the Sea of Azov and of the Black Sea. Into those seas three of the great rivers of Russia emptied themselves: there lay the peninsula of the Crimea, joined to the mainland by its narrow isthmus called the Perekop; and at the western end the opening known as the Bosphorus on which stood Constantinople. North and south of the Black Sea and in the Crimea the Turks had established themselves, with the earlier Mongol settlers as their vassals.

The story of the Turks on the Black Sea had

followed that of the Turks elsewhere in Europe. From the time of Peter the Great onwards Russia had sought to push back the alien occupants of the land, even as the more westerly powers had sought to press them back to the countries into which they had penetrated beyond Constantinople.

By 1768 progress had been made; but much remained to be accomplished. The particular aim of the successive rulers of Russia had been to reach the two seas, but despite some successes, and although the Sea of Azov had been reached and the river Don, emptying itself into that sea, had been freed or nearly so from Turkish rule, that rule, in the year when the struggle was about to recommence, was still supreme all around the Black Sea, and in its peninsula. And, since the Turks controlled the northern shore, they controlled likewise the lower reaches and the mouths of the three rivers, the Dnieper, the Bug, and the Dniester, which from east to west found their way to the Black Sea. To control the mouths of these rivers was to control the river trade. On every ground Turkey was the enemy, and experienced diplomats had long foreseen that sooner or later Russia would once more move against her. As far back as 1736 Horace Walpole had received a new map of the Crimea from Paris, with the remark that it had been drawn by a Russian. Walpole's comment had been that the eyes of the world were fixed on the line of the Perekop.

Yet, as it happened, it was Turkey, urged on by France in consequence of the happenings in Poland, who challenged Russia. Not that the challenge was a surprise either to Russia or to her fellow belligerent, Prussia. Both Catherine and Frederick had foreseen the possibility of Turkey's intervention in the matter of Poland, and some years earlier they had agreed that common action must be taken in Constantinople to avert such intervention, or if it could not be averted, then to turn it to account. As far as Catherine was concerned her method had been to set Russian agents at work not only in Constantinople, but in the Slavonic countries of the Balkans still occupied by Turkey. The work of those agents was to preach deliverance for the Slav people from their oppressors by the hand of Russia.

It was from the peninsula in the Black Sea, that, in the autumn of 1768, Turkey struck at Russia. The peninsula, known alternatively as the Crimea or Taurida or the Chersonese, had long been one of the best organized of the Mongol settlements, owning the Sultan of Turkey as its overlord. It was also one of the most prosperous; a prosperity based upon the wealth of the district in agriculture, in industry and in commerce. As the climate was favourable for agriculture, so the peninsula was geographically admirably suited as a trading centre, provided that the shores of the Black Sea with the river mouths were under the same control.

But if the Mongols of the Crimea were a well-organized settlement, they also retained much of their earlier character as raiders. With their fellows on the northern shore of the Black Sea they spent the winter of 1768 and the early spring of 1769 conducting a series of inroads into Russian territory. The inroads were of the kind which had long been terrifyingly familiar to the people among whom they came. Suddenly the invaders would appear in a district, riding, as they have been pictured, crouched like monkeys on their horses, moving with the swiftness of greyhounds, creating terror and confusion, killing, looting, taking prisoners, whose fate would be to feed the great slave markets on the far side of the Mediterranean; and then retiring as quickly as they had come, across the Perekop. That winter was an appalling one for the Russian dwellers on the frontier. The prisoners carried off numbered thousands; and the amount of booty taken matched the numbers of the prisoners. Little if any help came from St. Petersburg. The declaration of war by Turkey, although foreseen, had come before Catherine and her advisers were in complete readiness. Some of the best Russian regiments were with Suvorov in Poland. A good deal had to be done before the rest of the army should be ready for serious warfare. Help was, however, available in the immediate neighbourhood. Russia had her Cossacks, dwellers in the steppes beyond the Mongol-occupied territory.

Cossack was not a racial name. Rather it designated a manner of life. The call of the steppes had ever attracted men whose deliberate choice was for a free existence in the wilds. To such men were joined others, poverty-stricken gentry, runaway peasants and workmen and men of all classes who sought refuge from retribution for misdeeds; with the element of free-booting always present. The Cossack numbers, which were very large, were made up in the main of Russians; but also included were Poles and their kin as well as Swedes and Scots from the north; and even a proportion of Mongolians who sought other allegiance than that to the Sultan of Turkey. Together they formed a number of communities, of whom the three principal were the Cossacks of the Dnieper; those of the Don; and beyond, further yet to the east, those of the Ural river. At all times they were recruited in the capacity of irregular but most efficient cavalry soldiers. Their greater importance was, perhaps, the service they did Russia on the frontier. As good horsemen, as ardent fighters, and as skilled in guerilla and predatory tactics as were the Mongols themselves, the Cossacks conducted the border warfare in 1768 and 1769 as they had long conducted it, and the advantage was by no means always with the subjects of the Sultan.

So passed the winter. In the spring of 1769 Catherine was ready. She did not, however, move in the direction of the Crimea. That frontier fighting for the moment could be taken care of by the Cossacks. Her first blow was aimed at Turkey in the Balkan peninsula. Through that peninsula, the greater part of which had been occupied by the Turks since the early sixteenth century, ran the great water highway, the Danube with its tributaries, to empty itself, in its turn, into the Black Sea. Now Catherine made two bold strokes. The first was by land. In the spring of 1769 a Russian army, under a good leader, Prince Golitsyn, reached the river Dniester; defeated a Turkish army on its banks; and went on to occupy, first, Jassy, the capital of the Turkish province of Moldavia, and, then, Bucharest, the capital of their province of Wallachia.

This was sufficiently startling to Europe. The following year was to unfold a still more startling event. A Russian fleet appeared in the Mediterranean.

The work done during the past winter, and before, had not been confined to the army. There is evidence that the efficiency of the Russian navy had been much weakened since the great days of Peter the Great. Catherine herself had written to Panin that while Russia had ships and men, she did not, it would appear, possess a navy. That there must be reorganization had long been clear to her; and, in fact, some work had been done comparatively early in her reign. It was then that the Earl of Buckinghamshire had visited Cronstadt with her in order to survey the fleet lying in that harbour. His story is that on that occasion Catherine disputed with him as to which end of a man-of-war went out of the harbour first. The story may be true, revealing Catherine's self-confidence even when she had no knowledge of technical matters. But her powers of conception on broad lines were great; and she seldom failed to seize on the ideas of others and to make them her own.

In the navy, re-equipped, re-fortified and extended, three commanders were conspicuous. The one was Alexis Orlov. Neither of the other two were of Russian birth. Admiral John Elphinstone was one of the branch of that family who had settled in Russia. His colleague, Admiral Samuel Greig, had taken service in the Russian navy about the year 1763. Greig has been called the creator of the Russian navy. The parts played by the three respectively in the ensuing naval war have been diversely interpreted. That Orlov showed himself not unable is not disputed, nor that Elphinstone and Greig were sailors of experience.

Two contingents of the navy, one fleet under Elphinstone and the other under a Russian commander—not Orlov, who was to join them presently—left their bases, sailed through the Baltic and reached the North Sea. Authorities in France, hearing of the sailing, were both angry and alarmed. Had they been able to interfere they would have done so. They were not able;

and their opposing power, England, had no intention of putting any obstacle in the way of the passage of the ships. England did more than this. She permitted the vessels to revictual and to some extent refurnish at divers English ports. Thence the two fleets traversed the Atlantic to pass through the Straits of Gibraltar into the Mediterranean; making towards the Aegean Sea, with the Balkan peninsula jutting into it.

Here a project had been planned. Pursuant to the successes of the Russian army on land, an insurrection in Greece had been thought to be hopeful; and had been largely organized by Orlov, who, already in the Mediterranean, now joined the fleet. But the result was a complete fiasco; and for the Greeks a tragedy. Between February and May the latter were cruelly crushed by a united army of Turks and Albanians. The Russians could do nothing for them; and had every need to make ready to meet the Turkish fleet, whose sailors were experienced in every characteristic of the inland sea, so long the scene of their many exploits, including slave raids. It was a sea to which the Russians now came for the first time.

The great clash did not come until the month of July. In the first week of that month the two fleets met in a battle which was short and sharp. The Turkish fleet was not merely scattered; it was, by a final blow delivered off Chios, to all intents and purposes destroyed. The Russian fleet lay triumphantly at the eastern end of the Mediterranean. At the same time the Russian armies were in full occupation of Moldavia and Wallachia and had been hailed by the Orthodox population as an army of liberation.

During these two years of victories Catherine had never lacked the stimulus of admiration from at least one of her correspondents. From the moment when the great enterprises on land and afterwards at sea had begun, the old sage of Ferney had permitted himself to go into ecstasies; ecstasies which moved him to verses in which he saluted Catherine's coming triumph over Mohammed. Catherine was, so she was assured by Voltaire, a greater even than Hannibal had been. The philosopher imagined himself, so he wrote, no longer to be living in the eighteenth century, but to be back in the heroic age. Surely, he continued, her fleet, watched over and blessed by Hero and Leander, must triumph in the Hellespont. For to Voltaire, as to Catherine herself, the end of all was to be Constantinople.

The alarm, however, felt elsewhere than at St. Petersburg and on the shore of the lake of Geneva was profound. France, in using Turkey against Russia, had laid the match to a train of events, of which the consequences had now to be faced. All Europe had to ask the question whether they really desired to see Turkey driven out of Europe; leaving in its place Russia holding Constantinople and established on the Danube.

France had no choice but to continue her support of Turkey, even if she wished otherwise, which Choiseul was far from doing. French engineers, to whose skill the defences of Constantinople already owed much, were again working on the fortifications. Austria, for her part, had begun to re-arm. Maria Theresa now had a co-ruler in her son, who, as Joseph II, had succeeded his father in 1765 as Emperor. To both, and to their ministers, the penetration of Russia into the Balkans was even more disconcerting than had been the Turkish rule there. Of the great powers there remained England and Prussia.

England had not played a great part in continental diplomacy since the close of the Seven Years War. Nor did she, at this time, view the question of the eastern end of the Mediterranean as vital to her interests. Russia was not seen as a threat to India, where the East India Company now ruled triumphant after the conflict with France. Rather it was the latter country who was still England's rival and potential enemy. At any moment France might try to regain what had been lost; and it was France who was England's trade rival in the Mediterranean. Pitt, now Earl of Chatham, remarked for his part that as against Turkey he was quite a 'Russ', and expressed the hope that the fall of the Ottoman Empire would bring down with it the House of Bourbon. England further now had a great and important trade with Russia—as is shown by the records of the merchant vessels entering and leaving the mouth of the Neva. Economically she desired to keep that trade at all hazards. On her side, Catherine, frankly disliking the English parliamentary system and the constitution generally, valued her connections, both economic and political, with England; and was prepared to go some lengths—including on the one hand flattery and on the other the use of skilful Russian agents —to retain some sort of an understanding. She did, it is true, express the opinion that alliance with a parliamentary government was never likely to be of a durable nature. Durable alliances were not, however, she might have reflected, a feature of the day, whatever the nature of the government or governments involved. But neither England nor Russia was inclined to come into opposition one with the other.

There remained Prussia; and Frederick of Prussia proposed a solution of the situation. Frederick, by his own showing in his memoirs, did not in the least want to see Turkey wiped off the map of Europe. Austria had been his ancient enemy; and who could say whether Turkey might not at some future date be of service as against Austria? More than this. She could be similarly used as a check on Russia. He and Catherine were writing regularly one to the other; and the two countries had been acting together. But this was far from meaning that Frederick was prepared to take any risks in respect of the schemes of his correspondent, and the vast potentialities of the country over which she ruled. Strictly speaking he had been bound by treaty to assist Catherine in the war which had now broken out; but to see Turkey replaced by Russia at Constantinople was no part of his plans; nor had he any intention of being drawn into the conflict. There was another way out.

Already in the year 1768, the year of the formation of the Confederation of Bar and the beginning of war in Poland, he had written in what was to be his political testament, that the main object of policy for his successor should be to secure that part of Poland known as ducal Prussia, which had long been the subject of claims by the latter country. He added that the chief obstacle in the way was likely to be Russia; and that on the whole it would probably be advisable to attempt to annex the district bit by bit, by negotiations, rather than by war. As the course of affairs in Europe progressed he had not been slow to perceive that an opportunity now offered to carry out the desired plan himself, instead of leaving it to his successor; provided that it was made in the first place worth Russia's while; and in the next, Austria's, to acquiesce. Early in 1769 the Prussian Ambassador in St. Petersburg had been ordered to approach the Empress and also Count Panin. The Ambassador was to ascertain whether they would be inclined, in return for a slice of Poland, to allow Frederick to take his slice and, as a further consideration, to conclude a negotiated peace with Turkey.

Panin, even though he had long been in the pay of the Prussian King, had not been favourably impressed. He continued to hold the opinion that a strong Poland, well-affected to Russia, would best serve the latter's purpose. Catherine, on the other hand, had arrived at the point of being ready to go beyond her original policy with regard to Poland and had definitely been thinking, as had some among her advisers, in terms of an advance of the western frontier. She had showed herself, therefore, willing to consider what to her was a tempting and also practical proposition, the more so because she had not yet been in the full tide of the victories over Turkey, and had been alarmed at the war-like preparations in Austria.

Then Frederick, that 'honest broker', had turned to Austria; to Maria Theresa, in her early fifties a tired woman; to Joseph II; to the Chancellor Kaunitz. It was the two latter who, with the King of Prussia, brought pressure to bear on the former and her conscience, a conscience which, as she wrote to Kaunitz, told her what was being proposed was contrary to all justice. But, she had continued, as she saw she stood alone, and was lacking in her old strength, she must give in.

So the scheme progressed. In 1770, an envoy from Frederick, his brother Henry of Prussia, arrived in St. Petersburg, to leave for posterity a book of memoirs on his experiences there.

Catherine, since the first mooting of the matter, had had her triumphs on land and on sea. Yet, in this year, her conquests appeared to be static. Despite Voltaire's invocation of Hero and Leander, her navy had not penetrated the straits. Constantinople still stood. Nor had her army made any further really substantial advances on land. Moreover, news had come from Poland that the French had sent thither the general Dumouriez, known as a first-class soldier, who was to reorganize the forces of the Confederation. It was time to come to an agreement; and both the Empress and Panin were prepared to listen to Prince Henry, even though the minister never ceased to have his doubts—urging always, as before, the desirability of a strong, a free, a friendly Poland, as a buffer state.

The negotiations continued over another two years. During that time Poland, as so often in her history, experienced all the emotions of success and of failure. In April, 1771, Dumouriez led the forces of the Confederation—he had only a few French troops with him—to victory on the banks of the Vistula, when a Russian army was routed. Had he been able to follow up this triumph much might have been done, but the French general had found the Polish troops under his command difficult to deal with, nor was he on good terms with the leaders of the Confederation. After a defeat at the hands of Suvorov and his men, Dumouriez withdrew to his own country. The struggle then centred round Cracow, which fell to Suvorov in the spring of 1772. At the same time an Austrian as well as a Prussian army had assembled on their respective frontiers, ready to invade a country which now lay at their mercy. It was time to act. In August, 1772, the documents effecting what was to be known as the first Partition of Poland were signed. As the price of putting an end to the Russian-Turkish conflict, and, more particularly, of averting a general conflagration, Poland was to be stripped of about one-fourth of her territory. That fourth was now divided into three more or less equal divisions, taking population as well as territory into consideration. To Russia fell the portion east of the rivers Dwina and Dnieper: to Austria parts of Galicia, Podolia and Little Poland, with the city of Cracow. Frederick secured his coveted ducal Prussia but was forced, in spite of all efforts to the contrary, to acknowledge Dantzig and Thorn as independent.

In the truncated kingdom Stanislas Augustus remained king. And, since the Confederation of Bar was now, after the fall of Cracow, beaten to its knees, the Russian troops were, by agreement, withdrawn. The Russian agents, however, remained.

Since this partition, profoundly shocking such tender consciences as existed in the Europe of the day, a deed which was to be the subject of lofty invective by future writers, was intended to end the Turkish war, Gregori Orlov was despatched by Catherine to meet the Turks as her plenipotentiary. Orlov, she opined, since without exaggeration he was the most handsome man of the day, would appear to these barbarians in the guise of an angel. But the 'barbarians', perceiving that they held some useful cards, proposed to bargain with the angel. The discussions dragged on. Another meeting, in 1773, at Bucharest, brought equally poor results. Catherine lost patience. Against the advice of her commander in Wallachia she ordered the immediate reopening of hostilities and advance of the Russian forces. In face of the strongly entrenched Turkish positions, and the nature of the ground, the plan was, as her generals told her, extremely dangerous. In the event it was the incompetence of a Turkish commander —who paid for that incompetence with his head —which saved the Russian army from defeat, and perhaps from annihilation. There was some further fighting. But the Turks had had enough. Catherine too had warnings, which could not be ignored, of trouble within Russia itself. On 21 July, 1774, the treaty of peace was signed at Kuchuk-Kainardji.

The territorial clauses of this treaty seemed at first sight to offer Russia inadequate reward for the penetration of her armies westward beyond the Dniester, not to speak of her naval triumph in the Aegean, although this had not had the hoped-for results. The agreement now was that the Russian armies should withdraw completely from Moldavia and Wallachia. Acquisition of territory at the expense of Turkey was, however, provided for elsewhere: on the shores of the Black Sea where the Cossack forces, augmented by some regular troops, had fought with considerable success; and around the Sea of Azov. On the latter the much-disputed port of the same name passed finally into Russian hands; and so, too, to the south-east, beyond the Sea of Azov, did a part of the province of Kuban. More important, the town and fortress of Kerch guarding the narrow straits between the two seas was, with the adjacent district, a second-ary peninsula, handed over to Russia. Westward, although the Crimea remained under its Khan and the tributaries of Turkey along the northern shore of the Black Sea were merely declared independent, the great estuary formed by the Dnieper and the Bug as they entered the sea, with the town of Kinburn at the mouth of the former river, was declared Russian. Russia had obtained a firm footing on the northern shore of the Pontus Euxinus of the ancient world, the sea towards which so many of her rulers before Catherine had turned longing eyes. The footing was strengthened by further concessions which gave Russia rights of free passage for purposes of trade both on sea and on land with the Turkish dominions. It was a signal triumph. Yet jurists and diplomats of a later day were inclined to attach as much, if not more, importance to certain further clauses in the treaty. These latter concerned neither territory, nor trade, but the church for which Russia stood. Nor did they form one complete section of the document. On the contrary, they were scattered throughout various sections in a disorder which, as the French historian Sorel was afterwards to remark, did a great deal of credit to the diplomatic dexterity of Catherine's plenipotentiaries.

By these clauses the Turkish government promised that in future and in perpetuity all Christians living in the lands over which they held sway should be allowed freedom of worship; old churches might be repaired; new churches might be built. One such edifice was specifically mentioned. An Orthodox church was to be built in the Galata suburb of Constantinople for public worship as distinct from the private chapel of the Russian Ambassador, but also under his protection. Incidentally, the Russian embassy was now to be permanent at the Porte, which had not been the case hitherto. Lastly, the Turkish authorities undertook to receive in a friendly spirit all or any representations made in future by Russia on behalf of the Orthodox congregations.

Whatever the meaning the signatories of the treaty had intended should be attached to these stipulations, as to those dealing with trade, all very quickly acquired a wide interpretation. By virtue of them Russia was to put forward her claim to become the instrument of civilization within the Turkish dominions, and in so doing to claim also the right to intervene in the domestic affairs of that empire.

Catherine might be held to be justified when, in 1773, the year before the signing of the treaty, she had celebrated the Russian victories, not in St. Petersburg, but in Moscow, driving in the evening in a gilded coach to the Kremlin, where, in the Chapel of the Assumption, lit up by what an English traveller described as myriads of tapers, was held a solemn service of thanksgiving.

Nevertheless, in this same year of 1773, Catherine had been faced by a grave disturbance within Russia itself.

Chapter Seven

Pugachev

THE disturbance within Russia which occurred in the moment of triumph over Turkey had, at first, been regarded by the Empress and her ministers as tiresome, but of small import. It was some little time before they realized its gravity, and even so, only here and there a keen-eyed observer suspected the full significance of a rebellion which was to stand out among the many which had punctuated the course of Russian history.

It was no palace revolution. It was trouble in the vast territories of that Russia which lay beyond St. Petersburg; beyond Moscow. And it concerned the workers on the land and in industry.

Neither the establishment of the Free Economical Society nor the discussions of the Commission had brought any advantage to the peasants. On the contrary, the year 1765 had seen the landowners secure authority to send a recalcitrant serf to Siberia without either reference to the law or right of appeal. That latter right had once been possessed by the worker, even if only in theory. Now it had been completely wiped out. At the same time while some of the more enlightened landowners were inclined to do their best in easing general conditions for their peasants; under others, many of them alarmed at the talk of freedom, those conditions were growing worse. And there was revolt. Since the beginning of Catherine's reign disturbances had, it was reckoned, broken out on different occasions in at least fifty separate districts; and on at least two occasions had reached considerable dimensions.

Those disturbances had not been confined to workers on the land. Another class was as much in bondage as they; and was working under as bad, if not worse, conditions. Such were those who laboured in the factories, and in the mines; and to these must be added the woodmen and charcoal burners of the forests, not strictly speaking peasants. In all these cases the perennial shortage of labour had ended in the debasement of those who laboured, for the difficulty had been met, as in agriculture, by the creation of a system that was, in effect, forced labour, in mines, factories and forests, whether these were worked directly by the state, or were leased by the state to private owners; or were the property of the latter.

In the beginning, again, as had also been the case with the peasants, a certain number of free or unbonded men had worked side by side with others, who were unfree. Some of these latter belonged by status to the state or to private owners; others were bonded peasants of landowners who had been compulsorily transferred from agriculture; and yet others were conscripted convicts or deportees. All received fixed wages, with travelling allowances for those living away from their employment. All were liable for taxes; and here was an additional grievance; for the taxation was based on the individual only in theory. In practice it was based on the group; so that all payments due from absentees, whether these were runaways, or had been taken away by the authorities for military service, had to be made up by those who remained.

As time went on, the lot of these workers in industry ran parallel to that of the workers on the land. The free or partially free were gradually debased to the condition of their bound fellows, until an edict of 1736 took away all liberty of action, in providing that all workmen should remain each in his factory or mine, with his family, for ever. Whether their circumstances were even moderately tolerable depended upon the administration, and that administration differed widely from place to place. But travellers and observers during the last three decades of the eighteenth century seldom failed to record the often miserable condition of the workers, nor to note the inexpediency of obligatory labour; and the use made of it by the all too often unscrupulous employer, whether he were a private individual or some official.

Voices had been raised on behalf of those workers. Petitions had reached the authorities.

Catherine herself was as aware of the importance of the problem as she was aware of that of the workers on the land. She had had enquiries made. In 1769 she had decreed a rise of wages. The former had come to nothing. The latter had immediately been followed by a disconcerting rise in prices. Catherine was not averse to proposing reforms and some such reforms might have been effective had she been able to carry them through.

She was not so able. Her own dependence on the prejudices of those who had helped her to attain the throne and now were keeping her there; the very vastness of Russia, the unwieldy yet ancient machinery which the commission had done little or nothing to improve; the many conflicting interests; all were obstacles in the path of possible change. It was easier, almost necessary for even an autocrat Empress to leave things as they were. So, punctuated by outbursts, some light, some more ominous, among the peasants, and other workers, matters had continued. Then came serious trouble.

The area of disturbance was in that section of the steppes which lay south of a line drawn from east to west through Moscow; between the Don and the Ural rivers, and intersected by the Volga river. It was a land which was partly wooded and partly grass grown, the grass of the steppes, growing freely in the rich black soil. It was the land of great estates, their houses and their dependents. But the vast stretches of country, watered by the three great rivers, were also the background for other communities. On the western edge of the district were the Cossacks of the Don. While they retained many of their original characteristics, this particular community had, during the past century, gradually evolved from a completely wild life into a more settled one. Still sending many recruits to the army, they had also developed both agricultural and trading interests; and in these they had prospered to a remarkable degree; having many contacts with the world outside. Therein they were in marked contrast to the communities of the two rivers to the east, the Volga and the Ural. The district of the Volga, with its trading fortified posts, had a population which was a mixture of Mongol and Russian. That population, unlike those of the other two rivers, had never organized itself, or part of itself, into a regular Cossack host or community. But in the seventeen-seventies, the district was still, as it had long been, a happy hunting-ground for adventurers, vagrants, bands of marauders and river pirates. And, to the east, were Cossacks again, the Cossacks of the Ural river, who clung to the old wild life of the steppes; and who represented a far stronger Mongol element and a far more lawless one than did the Cossacks of the Don. Between the Volga and the Ural rivers was combustible material in plenty. And that combustible material was, comparatively speaking, in dangerously close proximity to a set of workers among whom discontent had been, and was, particularly rife.

To the north of the Ural river as it flowed westward from the Ural range before turning sharply southward towards the Caspian Sea, was the province of Orenburg. The principal town of the same name stood at the confluence of the Orel river with the Ural river. It was of great importance as a fortress; as a trading post with the Asiatic frontier; and as a centre for the many industrial settlements which had been founded in proximity to the Ural mountains, since that range had been reached by Russia early in the fifteenth century. Salt mines had been worked throughout the district, particularly in the neighbourhood of Orenburg, from the earliest days. Under Peter the Great had come a development of the iron and copper industries. At the same time the forests, in which the district also abounded, had offered opportunities, which had been taken, for fur trading; for the lumber industry which was so essential; and the charcoal making which was as essential to almost every other industry. The Urals had, too, an almost inexhaustible supply of salt, a monopoly of the crown, both rock salt and that drawn from salt lakes. Lastly there was a flourishing silk trade, which had derived from Persia whence came silkworms and the mulberry trees which supplied their food.

All these industries were either in the hands of the crown or had been given over for development to various great merchant families. The lot of those who worked in them, particularly in respect of the mining district of the Urals, a lot of slavery, was probably as bad as, if not worse than, could be found anywhere else in Russia. Taken in conjunction with the grievances of the peasants on the great estates to the south and the south-east, there existed every potentiality for a conflagration. In 1771, the industrial workers and peasants alike were approached by an adroit agitator; and the smouldering material began to blaze up.

The agitator in question was Emilian Pugachev, a Cossack, not however of the Ural river but of the Don; not one of the more law-abiding kind of that community. Interested neither in agriculture nor trade, Pugachev had early become one of the irregular horsemen attached to the regular army; and had fought in Poland and in Turkey. As a soldier his career had been punctuated by a series of conflicts with authority; followed by spells of imprisonment. From the last of these he had escaped; had made his way back to the steppes, but not to his own community on the Don. He had appeared instead, in the year 1771, among the Cossacks of the Ural. In that community always more or less in antagonism to authority, he had quickly made himself a figure round whom all who had grievances, all who were disposed to rebellion, rallied. Thence the flame of revolt spread to the workers and peasants whose grievances in their turn were fanned by clever manifestos sent forth by Pugachev, although probably not composed by him.

Catherine and her advisers in St. Petersburg, and in Moscow, were not at first unduly perturbed by the news of what was happening; although Moscow may well have felt more acutely on the subject than did the northern capital. The older capital had experienced much in the past of which Peter's city knew nothing. But Catherine, writing to Voltaire, even in January, 1773, referred to the disturbances as one of the only too familiar Cossack revolts. This impudent Pugachev was, she wrote, merely a common highwayman; and the population of the district in which he had appeared consisted for the most part of Tartars, whom everyone knew to have been pillagers ever since the world was created; and joined with these every rascal, of whom the more civilized part of Russia had seen fit to rid itself during the last forty years. She personally did not intend that the news of the rising should disturb the intercourse, in which she was taking so much pleasure, with Diderot, who was at that moment on his second visit to St. Petersburg. Voltaire in reply agreed that the conversation between Catherine and one of the princes of the encyclopædists ought in no wise to be impeded by the exploits of a brigand.

It was not long before Catherine at least was to perceive that something more than brigandage was in question; and in that same letter to

Voltaire, she had already mentioned a fact of some significance. The impertinent fellow was, she wrote, actually calling himself by the name of, and claiming to be, the late Emperor, her one-time husband, Peter III.

So Pugachev had indeed given forth. The Emperor, it was explained, had not been killed after all. On the contrary, he had escaped, and gone on his travels in Poland, in Egypt, or, according to one version, had even reached Jerusalem.

The path of pretender has always been open to all adventurers in all lands; and this resurrection of Peter in particular was not in itself a new idea. Four previous pretenders at least, also calling themselves by Peter's name, had already appeared, and had been dealt with. But under Pugachev the play was made much more elaborate. The sumptuous background included a court, a secretary of state, a queen, and an heir. It all partook of the nature of fantasy; by a further touch of which an Orlov and a Vorontsov were included among the staff.

Pugachev's more intelligent supporters could never have had any doubt that the man who claimed to be Emperor was, in fact, a typical Cossack, of striking character, but almost illiterate, and many years younger than the man he claimed to be; and that his so-called queen was a Cossack girl from the Urals. Incidentally, the latter was not even Pugachev's legal wife, for he had left

another, with a family of children, in the district of
the Don. But the appeal was a subtle one, for it
was made to something even over and above that
in human nature which is called forth by a pretender, any pretender. It was an appeal to the
feeling, half filial, half mystical, entertained by
the average Russian towards his Tsar. Their
Little Father, could he but hear them, would
redress their grievances. That this particular
Little Father, having been said to have been
dead—and many may not have heard of the
death—should thus reappear as their saviour,
was not astonishing. The dweller in the great
forests or in the steppes was essentially one
who could accept strange happenings, since
in his experience of nature such did occur. All
this was backed by something more solid. What
had never been forgotten was that when Peter III
had issued his edict which had released the
gentry from their obligation of service, it had
been spread abroad that this edict had been
intended to be the forerunner of another. And
that this other would emancipate the serfs.
Many had even said that the second edict had
actually been drawn up and had then been
suppressed. Now Pugachev, whether of his own
volition, or as advised by some of those around
him, made good use of this lost edict; and
appealing thus in the name of Peter III, the
Cossack called for support from all who wished
to redeem their lot.

158

By November in 1773 he had got together a considerable force. His own Cossack troops might be irregulars, but they were also in many cases men of considerable trained military experience; not to speak of their own aptitude for guerilla warfare. These men were ready and willing to train for service the workers from the mines, the factories, the forests, and the land generally who flocked to join the host. One weak point, however, was the almost complete abstention of the Cossacks of the Don, the district from which Pugachev had originally come; and moreover, the district which had for many years supplied the best fighting men to the Russian armies. The abstention marked clearly the difference which had grown up between this community and the Cossacks of the Ural and their neighbours.

Towards the end of the month Pugachev made his first move. He proceeded to invest the town of Orenburg and at the same time his men spread themselves over the surrounding district; inviting everywhere co-operation from all workers.

In the meantime, the authorities in St. Petersburg and Moscow had become aware of the new activities of this highwayman; and, although still not at the moment disposed to take it as anything more than one of the disturbances with which they were already familiar, they saw that something must be done. A general named

Karr was instructed to proceed with a body of troops towards Orenburg, and to quell the revolt. Karr was the Russian version of Ker or Carr. The general was one of the numerous Scotsmen who during the past two centuries, and even before, had been exercising many professions, civil as well as military, in Russia. In Russian records he was usually referred to as having come from North Britain. He may well have been a descendant of that Robert Ker, a Scottish soldier of fortune, who had been prominent in Russia during the early part of the seventeenth century. If of the Scottish border family, the general might have been supposed to be particularly suited to deal with such an insurrection as that of Pugachev appeared to be. But St. Petersburg had entirely underrated the strength of the movement which he was sent to face. Karr and his troops reached the Orenburg district to find Pugachev's men far more numerous, far better trained and far better armed than had been imagined could be the case; and daily they were being reinforced by workers, peasants and others, continuing to arrive in a regular stream. At the same time the rebels had the supreme advantage of being in many cases native to the district in which they were fighting. And at their back another movement was taking place, which, if it only helped them to a lesser degree, was considerable additional trouble to Karr's army. This was the emergence of a number of bands of robbers, and river pirates from the Volga, whom the news of the insurrection had released from the very light restrictions that they had ever put upon themselves.

It was small wonder that in the district around Orenburg all should have been tumult and affright among the gentry who saw the threat to their property, and as they knew well, to their own lives. Something very like a mass retreat to Moscow began among them.

Into the turmoil came Karr and his men; only to find that they were quite insufficient to attack Pugachev's forces; or even to hold their own. Karr returned to Moscow; made a report; and was dismissed by Catherine for having left his post without leave. But the month was now January; and enough had been learnt for Catherine and her ministers to see that the situation could not be played with. It was decided to replace Karr by General Bibikov, he who had presided over the commission. So that no time should be wasted large numbers of infantry were sent off in post carts as a preliminary instead of being marched.

Before Bibikov himself left for the front, Catherine summoned a council. One purpose of the meeting was to have the instructions to the general read aloud, himself present. But the manifesto which embodied those instructions contained something more; and that something was creditably said to have been the inspiration of Catherine herself. It was her answer to the claim of Pugachev to be no Cossack rebel, but to be Peter III, returned from exile. In her reply, she, who had taken Peter's place, bade those assembled to look back to the days, the terrible days as she called them, of Boris Godonov. Then, too, the throne, she declared, had been threatened as it was being threatened today, by a pretender, who had claimed to be the late Tsarevitch Demetrius; one who had plunged Russia into civil war, the blood of Russia shed by Russians, and set towns and villages all aflame.

It is noteworthy that Gregori Orlov and others as well are said to have asked for the deletion of the reference to the man who two hundred years before had seized the throne of Russia, without a vestige of hereditary claim, the true heir having supposedly been murdered with or without his cognizance. That Catherine should so have used the story throws, perhaps, some light upon the mind of the woman who had convinced herself of the righteousness of her destiny. Her correspondent at Ferney looked at the matter from yet another angle. Catherine received a letter from him in February; an answer to hers which had informed him of the revolt. In his he thanked her for transporting him in spirit to Orenburg, and for making him acquainted with Monsieur Pugachev. He added that hitherto he had always believed, from his reading of Persian history, that the district in which the highwayman was operating was a most favoured land. Now he learned from

the letter of the Empress that it was on the contrary a barbarous country filled with vagabonds
and criminals. Catherine, however, must remem-
ber that her rays, although as of the sun, could not
penetrate everywhere at the same time; and the
furthest confines of an empire that extended over
2,000 miles in longitude could only be dealt with
from a distance. As for Pugachev calling himself by the name of the late Emperor; and the
analogy of Demetrius; that kind of theatrical
performance, wrote Voltaire, might have been
successful two hundred years ago, but surely
today it could be whistled away. So spoke the
authoritative voice of the age of reason.

In the meantime Bibikov, having received his
instructions, had left. A not unimportant clause
in those instructions had told him to attack with
that superiority which always belongs to a disciplined army against a mob moved only by emotion
and fanaticism. This was sound enough. But
Bibikov had no delusions about the difficulty of
his task. His early contacts with the situation as
he found it on his arrival at the Orenburg front
made him take an even more serious view of what
was going on. He sent a report to St. Petersburg.
That report stated that Pugachev himself really
mattered very little. But, added Bibikov flatly,
the universal discontent mattered very much. The
importance of the Cossack was that he had now
become a symbol; and the revolt which he was
leading had become a widespread peasant move-

ment. It was, wrote the general, a revolt of the
poor against the rich.

Bibikov had, indeed, summed up the situation
correctly. Further, it now became evident that
Pugachev was getting more support from somewhat unexpected quarters. Many of the regular
troops had their own grievances, which spurred
them on to make common cause with the rebels.
Also, to the surprise of many onlookers, it became
clear that the movement had the sympathy of the
clergy, that is of those priests who were most
closely in touch with the peasantry, and remote
from the hierarchy of Moscow and St. Petersburg.
That hierarchy, on the whole, stood by the crown,
and so did, as a rule, the monastic orders.

Throughout the spring months the campaign
continued. In spite of more than one defeat at
the hands of Bibikov's men the Cossack held his
own; and more than his own. Not only was he
successful in the field, but his influence and consequently the movement of revolt continued to
spread northward through the provinces of Ufa
and Perm and north-westward through Samara.
Workers from the further off salt and copper mines
came into the capital of the province of Perm to
listen eagerly to the manifestos which promised
redress of all their grievancs. Abandoning their
employment they thronged with others to join
Pugachev. They looted and they sacked wherever
they went; while Pugachev as guerilla leader
deployed his troops so as wherever possible to

avoid giving battle to his more experienced opponents; but fighting whenever he had to fight.

By the end of June the movement to the north-west, the most ominous line taken by the insurgents, for it pointed straight at the heart of Russia, had approached the city of Kazan. On 12 July the rebel forces stormed the town, reducing it to a mass of blazing ruins. Standing on the Volga some fifty miles above the junction of that river with its tributary the Kama, Kazan had been a Mongol city until it had been seized in 1552 by Ivan the Terrible and incorporated in Russia, although the population had remained for the most part eastern and non-Russian. But, as Russia had pushed eastwarɑ, so had the economic importance of Kazan grown, in its connections with the Ural district, and in its comparative proximity to the Kama river which was the water-highway leading to Siberia. Now once more it suffered the fire and slaughter not unknown in its past history. Small wonder that Moscow, receiving panic-stricken refugees day after day, was terrified. At any moment it was felt Pugachev might appear at its gates. He, continuing to announce himself as Peter III, had declared his intention of disposing of the Empress, when he could get her, not by murder but by sending her to a convent, that time-honoured expedient for disposing of unwanted women. It was an expedient to which the regent Anne had been forced to submit by Elizabeth and other royal ladies before her, for the same fate had overtaken a too strong-minded sister of Peter the Great himself.

But there was to be no convent for Catherine and Pugachev never reached Moscow. General Bibikov died. But he was replaced by a good soldier, Peter Panin, a brother of the minister; and Panin had with him an excellent general, Mikhelson. On 15 July the latter caught up with and defeated Pugachev's forces just outside Kazan, where they had encamped. The defeat might have been fatal to the Cossacks then and there, had Mikhelson but had an efficient body of cavalry with him. His forces, however, consisted for the most part of infantry. Pugachev and many of his men, with their horses, got away. They even partially re-formed, to attempt a last desperate move to reach Moscow. But that move was a failure. The getting together of the men again was very far from complete. And now the essential weakness of the guerilla troops against a disciplined army became evident. More and more the former tended to break up into small bands; and more and more was the central authority over them weakened. At no time perhaps had Pugachev ever had full control over all who called themselves his followers. In August another notable regular general appeared on the scene. It was Suvorov, released from his service on the Polish and Turkish fronts. But when Suvorov came the rebellion was nearly over. On 22 October (2 November, N.S.), Catherine wrote to Voltaire that the Cossack had been captured a month since in the plain between the Volga and the Jaick rivers.

He had, she told her correspondent, admitted that he was in reality a Cossack of the Don, and had given his birthplace and the story of his marriages. There was, she further reported, no sign of his having been the instrument of any outside power. This supposition had been mentioned by Voltaire; and, in point of fact, there appears to be little doubt that Pugachev had been used by abler men than himself. In this letter Catherine insisted that he was merely a bold, brave and determined, but illiterate man, a master bandit whom, however, in his excesses and cruelties she likened to that great figure, Tamerlane. To this Voltaire replied that this devil of a man had then this in common with Genghis-Khan and Tamerlane, that none of the three could write. But, he continued, it was always said that there were persons who, without even being able to sign their own name, had founded religions. This, wrote the sage, was not to the honour of human nature. It was the magnanimity of Catherine which now did that nature honour. Voltaire was referring to Catherine's refusal, after Pugachev, described as a beaten, an abject, a timorous figure, had been brought to Moscow in a kind of cage, to allow torture to be used on him.

To have used torture would have been, for

those of her ministers who proposed it, the normal and natural proceeding. But even as her predecessor, Elizabeth, in her day, had objected to the employment of torture, so also did Catherine, and there is no reason but to believe that the sentiments she, not once but frequently, expressed on the subject were genuine. Long since, when she had heard of the tortures inflicted upon Robert Damien after his attempt on the life of Louis XV, she had written to Sir Charles Hanbury-Williams that the treatment of that wretched man was so horrible that it had made her hair stand on end. She had expressed something of the same feeling in her memoirs when speaking of the function of Peter Shuvalov as torturer general, he being head of the secret chancellery. And she had been as vehement as Voltaire in the indignation they had expressed to one another at the cruelties inflicted upon La Barre and Juan Calas when they had flouted the church. Something must be allowed for Catherine's perpetual insistence, particularly in her correspondence with Voltaire and others, upon her elevation of thought. But it is at least probable she really disliked torture. She was also too shrewd not to be aware of its effect upon public opinion.

There was, in fact, no need for drastic measures. Pugachev had had his hour. But the rebellion had failed; and in defeat, awaiting execution, he was a pitiful figure. He had never been of the stature of a Genghis or a Tamerlane, to whom

Catherine and Voltaire had likened him; nor had he attained that of a great national leader. It was General Bibikov who had seen his true importance. Pugachev had appeared as a flaming symbol; and was to go down in history as one; a symbol of forces that would eventually bring about the collapse of the Russian social system of the days of Catherine.

But those incipient forces were, for the time being, driven underground. The terror excited by the news of the movements of Pugachev's men, particularly in the districts east and south of Moscow, with their traditional memories of the coming of Mongol hordes, was very real; while government and landowners, horrified at the political implication of the rebellion, hardened their hearts and drew together in defence of both against serfdom. Almost everywhere, in the subsequent years, the lot of the worker grew harder.

Chapter Eight

Potemkin—The Crimea—Turkey

IN 1776 there arrived in St. Petersburg, as English Ambassador, Sir James Harris, afterwards Earl of Malmesbury. Sir James had previously been envoy in Berlin and his despatches from that capital had revealed his capacity for receiving and conveying impressions of persons and situations. His reports from Russia were of equal or even greater value in the pen pictures given of Catherine, the court and the policies pursued. In the Empress he saw much of what his predecessors had seen: the impressive bearing of a woman who had no claims to real beauty; the dignity and yet ease of manner; the power of pleasing; and the ability behind the determination to govern. But, arriving in Russia at a time when Catherine had reached her late forties, Harris perceived, and implied that others had perceived, deterioration in the Empress. Vanity and arrogance, fed by constant flattery and adulation, often taking the subtle form of homage offered to her intellect and her character, had been doing their work. And to these had been added the intoxication of success. Harris saw, in the triumph of the Polish adventure, something which had wrought damage in Catherine, for which he also blamed the influence of Frederick of Prussia. Lastly, in his analysis, the English Ambassador remarked on the coarsening which had come about as the result of immorality. Here he did not altogether agree with his predecessor, the Earl of Buckinghamshire, who had had no high opinion of Orlov and had expressed his disapproval of the submission of the Empress, when the affair was over, to what he called the ill-bred inattention of her former lover. Sir James, on the other hand, believed that on the whole the influence of Orlov had been for good. He reserved his condemnation for that of the extraordinary man who, in the years immediately before his own arrival in St. Petersburg, had become the principal figure at court and in the life of Catherine. The influence of Potemkin was, wrote Harris to England, a bad influence.

Gregori Potemkin was a Lithuanian, born in 1739, near Smolensk. After being educated at the university of Moscow he had entered a regiment of the guards, and, as one of them, had helped to ensure Catherine's safety on 28 June, 1762. For his services, he, like others, had been given a small estate. In 1768 he had become a gentleman of the household. But he was still a quite inconspicuous figure when, the following year, he quitted the court to take his part in the fighting on the Turkish front. Two years later he was once more at the court, and established as favourite of the Empress.

Of all those who won that favour, Potemkin, whether or no Sir James Harris was right in his conclusions, has been seen as the most romantic, the most outstanding figure. It was he around whom, more than any other man at Catherine's court, legends were to gather. A man of huge build, he was to go down into history as a cyclops —the story that he lost the eye in a duel with Orlov has probably no foundation in fact. He was thirty-four years of age when his connection with Catherine began. She was forty-four. As she had done before, she had chosen a lover younger than herself. Of the abilities of that lover, estimates varied. Some saw him as a good soldier and an even better administrator. Others judged him to be a man of medium attainments carried to fame by his personality. Indubitably the glamour of that personality was to continue down the ages, even as it had exercised its fascination over the Empress of Russia, not an inexperienced woman when she took him as her lover. In her—and his—softer moments he was addressed in the letters she sent him, letters written sometimes in Russian, sometimes in French, as her pigeon, her little one, her darling: all the array of affectionate diminutives used with particular effect in the Russian as in the French tongue. But, were he angry, he became her muscovite, her cossack, her ghiaour. And in his splendour he was her golden pheasant. The letters, intimate, revealing, were by no means confined to the times when the two were absent from one another. On the contrary, notes were sent to him daily, and sometimes more than once a day, when both were at Tsarskoe Selo, where only the ground saloon, later known from its decoration as the Chinese room, separated their apartments; or in the Winter Palace, where it is thought Potemkin occupied the suite of rooms immediately behind those of the Empress.

This same period of the seventeen-seventies saw other developments in Catherine's domestic circle. They, too, had their significance, even though not shot through with the changing fiery colours which lit up her intercourse with the lover. Catherine's son, the Grand-duke Paul, had reached years of maturity.

The boyhood of the Grand-duke can hardly have held much happiness. The attitude of his mother towards him was ever conditioned by recollections of the past: the talk of a regency; the shouts for the boy at her coronation. Here was something which might, in moments of crisis, spring to life again. On his side, always kept in the background, the Grand-duke had justification for resentment against the masterful Empress-mother to whom he was heir when he should have been Emperor. It seems clear that there was no affection between the two to soften the situation; and certainly Paul himself was hardly, according to all accounts, a pleasing person. But he was there. He was the heir. And the line must be carried on. In 1773, the Grand-duke, being then seventeen years of age, was married to a Princess of Hesse-Darmstadt. The wedding had a particular interest of its own in that Grimm came to Russia in the train of the bride, thus, like Diderot, making the personal contact with Catherine which Voltaire never made. But the marriage in itself proved none too successful. In 1776 the unhappy little Grand-duchess died in childbirth, leaving no son. Within five months Catherine had arranged a second marriage. Again a German Princess was chosen, this time from Wurtemberg, and this union gave Paul perhaps happiness he had not hitherto known. For his mother the events of supreme importance were the births of her grandsons. The elder, born in 1777, was named Alexander. Following on her years of triumph, the name had significance enough. When on 27 April (8 May, N.S.), 1779, a second son followed, the name bestowed upon him was even more significant. He was christened Constantine, a child, so the Empress told the English Ambassador, destined to a brilliant future. The medal struck to commemorate the birth showed on the one side the church of St. Sophia in Constantinople, on the other the Black Sea, and over the sea, a star. The eyes of the Empress-grandmother were indeed turning, more eagerly even than before, towards the Bosphorus.

It was in December, 1777, that Voltaire, an old man of eighty-three, had closed a letter to

Catherine with the cry: allah, allah, Catherine rezoul, allah! Six months later he lay dead in Paris. Participation in the fantasy which hung about the cradle of Constantine had not been for him. But that fantasy had emanated from something that was solid. Catherine had no longer the stimulus of Voltaire's letters, his visions of Hero and Leander. She had, however, by her side, a most eager coadjutator. By 1779 Potemkin, ceasing to be the lover, had stepped into the part of complaisant friend, and more than complaisant, for he not only tolerated but chose Catherine's lovers, her very young lovers, for her. His influence he was always to retain. That same year Sir James Harris reported that Count Potemkin was supreme in the court circle and entirely directed it. He, himself, he wrote in another letter, judged it best to try to work through him. As for Catherine's personal feeling for him, she appeared, when he was seriously ill in 1780, like a deranged creature. Potemkin was the all-important friend and adviser, who—there seems to be no doubt on this point— was not merely supporting the imperial plans out of policy, but was himself swept away by the vision of a new Empire for Russia, an Empire whose capital should be either Constantinople or Athens.

The vision found little or no favour with Panin. But that minister was fast ceasing to be of consequence. Potemkin, reported Harris, hated him; he was growing old; and apart from Potemkin,

he had a rival in Alexander Bezborodko, who had
become one of Catherine's personal secretaries
in 1775. Bezborodko, who had been educated at
Kiev, was an able administrator, a good historian
and the friend of Potemkin. The best Panin could
do was to keep in close touch with Frederick,
by whom he was still being paid. But Catherine,
again reported Harris, was growing tired of the
King of Prussia. This was hardly a surprise to
Frederick. His own remark had been that he never
expected fidelity from Catherine, since that virtue
was not her strong point. But in these last years
of his reign he still thought of an alliance with
Russia as necessary. Catherine was by no means
so sure that it was necessary for her. It was
Austria, not Prussia, whose lands were adjacent
to Turkey in Europe; she perceived that if she
were to accomplish her plans, she must come to
terms with Austria.

One happening, which had occurred two years
earlier, helped her much. A dispute had arisen
concerning the succession to Bavaria. One claim-
ant was Joseph of Austria, by reason of his
marriage with the sister of the late Elector. His
claim was opposed by Frederick, who had long
since remarked that that young man's actions
would bear watching and who in any case had
no desire to see Austria united with Bavaria under
one crown. When France refused help to
Austria, it seemed as if Joseph must yield. Maria
Theresa appealed to Catherine. The latter,

jointly with France, secured for Austria by the Arbitration of Teschen in May, 1779, that part of Bavaria known as the Quarter of the Inn. It was not all Joseph had claimed and desired, but it was an important, even if small, accretion to Austrian territory.

For Catherine, Teschen was a notable event; a recognition of the position to which she and the country over which she ruled had attained in the politics of Europe. It had further shown her as supporting Austria against Prussia. When, therefore, in pursuit of her own plans she made an approach to Joseph, she found him ready to listen. There was other common ground between the two. The Emperor, like the Empress of Russia, had sat at the feet of the philosophers and encyclopædists. As an enlightened despot, he had declared that philosophy must be the legislator of his empire.

In the late autumn of the same year Catherine was writing a series of letters to Joseph in which there was dangled before him the prospect of a visit to Russia. The idea gave Joseph, interested in and even fascinated by Catherine and her Russia, pleasure. It gave considerably less pleasure to Maria Theresa. That Empress was more than doubtful what might be the consequences to Austria of the visit. But 'the Mama', to use the title by which reference was made to her, was a failing woman, with only a year to live: and her son was gradually asserting his mastery of the situation and of her.

In the last week of May, 1780, Catherine, with Potemkin and Bezborodko in her train, went to Molihev in Lithuania, a town which had passed to Russia in the partition of 1772. Thither came the Emperor, travelling as Count Falkenstein. After five days the two imperial personages proceeded to Smolensk. Thence Catherine returned to the capital, while Joseph went to Moscow. A few days later he was received in state in St. Petersburg. He had no reason to complain of the reception. Catherine had made great preparations and the visitor, greeted with a profusion of illuminated emblems—always pleasing to the populace as well as to the visitor—was entertained as the court of Russia knew how to entertain an honoured guest. Lodged at Tsarskoe Selo, this guest was enchanted with everything, and found that the city of St. Petersburg, but more particularly the Winter Palace and the Hermitage, far surpassed his expectations. On his side he had already made a favourable impression. Catherine wrote to Grimm that she found her visitor both cultured and intelligent, and, she was pleased to say, a great reader of whatever he would, whether it were free-thinking literature or not. The book especially mentioned was that volume of Buffon's natural history, the *Epoques de la Nature*, which had appeared the previous year. But of what had passed between the pair Grimm received no more than hints. Nor had anything been made public when, at the end of July, the Emperor took his

leave. It was, however, well known that the
Turks were thoroughly alarmed and were making
great military preparations; while Harris, who
conveyed this information to England, also wrote
that he personally believed that the coming
together of Catherine and Joseph had struck a
blow at the influence of the King of Prussia from
which there would be no recovery. Frederick
himself, although Prussia attempted reassurance,
had already become sufficiently uneasy to ask
Catherine to receive his heir, the Prince Frederick
William, in St. Petersburg. The visit took place
in September, and was not a success.

In the meantime, Catherine and Joseph
were once more engaged in correspondence.
Maria Theresa was still doubtful of the wisdom
of Austria becoming involved in what she saw
were the far-reaching plans of Russia. But for
her the end was now very near. She died in
November, and her death left Joseph completely
free to do what he would. It was not, however,
until the following June that an understanding
concerning Turkey was arrived at by letter
between him and Catherine; and it was more than
a year later again, in September, 1782, that
Catherine finally formulated and put forward the
plan for the expulsion of the Turks from Europe
and the disposal of Turkey in Europe. On her
side it was a threefold plan. The frontier of
Russia was to be advanced from the estuary of
the rivers Dnieper and Bug, to which it had been

brought by the treaty of Kuchuk-Kainardji, as far westward as the river Dniester. Beyond the Dniester the provinces of Moldavia, Bessarabia and Wallachia were to be erected into a kingdom to be called, harking back to imperial Rome, the kingdom of Dacia; with Potemkin as Prince-ruler. The third and final demand was for an empire for Constantine, of which the capital should be Constantinople and which should include Thrace, Macedonia, Bulgaria, Albania and Northern Greece. Guarantees that this empire should never be united with Russia under one crown were promised. Austria, for her share, was to receive Serbia, Bosnia-Herzegovina and Dalmatia. The latter province was not part of Turkish territory but was held by the republic of Venice, which was to be asked for its cession in return for the Morea and either Cyprus or Crete.

As Joseph could not but perceive, the scheme offered Austria much. Here was the opportunity, with the aid of a powerful ally, to push the Turks back once and for all from the lands into which their hordes had penetrated; to extend the Austrian Empire into those provinces; and to replace the Moslem mosques by churches of the Roman communion. But he also did not fail to see that, though the actual territory to be acquired by Russia was, comparatively speaking, modest in extent, there was no modesty at all about the creation of the kingdom for Potemkin and the

Empire for Constantine. And who could say
what would be the course of future events were
these projects fulfilled, or what would be the consequences to Austria? Joseph, out of reach of the
personal influence of Catherine, saw with regard
to Austria what Frederick had seen with regard
to Prussia: that the interests of his country were
not in all circumstances identical with those of
Russia. Negotiations were begun. But no treaty
was signed. Apart from Joseph's hesitancy over
some of the provisions, there also intervened the
difficulty, a difficulty which had occurred before
in the history of Europe, of the matter of precedence. Joseph was not in the least inclined to abate
his claim to be the only Emperor in Europe, he
who stood for the Holy Roman Empire. Catherine, with the imperial title still comparatively
new in Russia, but a title the meaning of which
was as significant to her as to the man who had
adopted it, was not prepared to take second place,
even in a document. Nevertheless, to quote Mr.
Holland Rose, the two most daring rulers in
Europe had come to an understanding which
foreboded a general upheaval.

That that general upheaval was momentarily
delayed was due to Catherine's insistence on a
breathing space. In this she may well have had
to combat the impetuosity of her lieutenant. In
many quarters it was thought that Potemkin had
had the principal hand in drawing up the plan,
which, by reason of its third and most significant

proposal, was known as the Greek Project. Whether this were so or not, it was such as to meet with his ardent approval; and an equally ardent wish that it should be at once implemented. Catherine knew that there was much to be done in the way of preparation, military and naval within Russia and diplomatic without, before an effective move could be made.

But she and Potemkin had long had another plan, a supplementary plan, in mind; and this could be, and was, proceeded with. The treaty of Kuchuk-Kainardji had left the Crimean peninsula in the ambiguous position of being under Turkish rule, yet with a kind of nominal independence. Russia, however, had taken care that there should be infiltration of a great deal of Russian influence. By 1782 the Khan had become little more than a weak puppet of that country. Sometime early in 1783 complete annexation of the peninsula had been decided upon, and Potemkin had probably already had his secret instructions. He did not, however, immediately proceed south. It is possible that Panin had uttered some remonstrances. But on 11 April (22 April, N.S.), Harris wrote to England that Panin had, that same morning, died of apoplexy; and added that it was now said that Prince Potemkin would certainly leave at once for the Crimea. This was so. Potemkin, with his men, began operations around the Black Sea and across the Perekop early in May. The ground had been well prepared;

and there was little serious opposition. On 21 July, 1783, an official proclamation announced that the Tauride Peninsula was now part of the Russian Empire. In the next year the cession was acknowledged by Turkey.

Potemkin entered on his great epoch. He may already have been given estates within the recently acquired district known as the Ukraine. It is certain that he now became one of the great landowners in that fertile region of the good black earth; with gardens—laid out by a gardener brought from England—surrounding his house that even after his death were to be quoted as the wonder of southern Russia.

From these estates he directed what was nothing more nor less than a reconstruction of the surrounding regions, and of the peninsula of the Crimea itself. The exact personal responsibility for that work must always remain a matter of surmise, depending on the view of Potemkin's ability. That he was a conspicuous figure throughout is evident. He also, however, had the help of experts. Among them was Professor Pallas of Berlin, learned in the natural sciences, who some years earlier had been invited to St. Petersburg by Catherine, and who now, with estates of his own in the Ukraine, was established as scientific adviser in the reorganization that was taking place.

Both in the Ukraine and in the Crimea the nature of the soil and the geographical situation offered great possibilities for the development on the one hand of agriculture, and on the other of trade and commerce. Both branches of work were fostered; and two hindrances which might have stood in the way were overcome. The more lawless of the Cossacks had been partly but by no means completely subdued after the rebellion of Pugachev; they still remained a threat to law and order. As far as possible settlement was encouraged on the lines that had already been adopted, of their own free will, by the Cossacks of the Don; the Cossack regiments were also encouraged; and if the discipline became stricter, the men composing those regiments retained much of their individuality, as did also those who settled on the land. Punitive expeditions dealt with the wilder elements, of whom the survivors largely fled into and across the Caucasus, and the adjacent regions. But for effective development much labour, both agricultural and industrial, was required; and that labour was in great part lacking. To remedy this in the first instance a system of colonization, both free and forced, was pursued. Groups, mainly of the Slavonic race, were brought from Austria and elsewhere. A number of German colonies were also founded. After this, ordinary labour was supplied by the introduction of serfdom, as it prevailed elsewhere but to which the Ukraine had hitherto been a stranger.

But no one knew better than Catherine and her advisers that defence against enemies from without had to be provided. The southern shore of the Black Sea was still held by the Turks; even as they held at the western end the narrow strait that was the Bosphorus; and Constantinople. The western shore too, was the frontier of Turkey in Europe; and, on the northern shore, that frontier still extended as far as the river Dnieper. But on the estuary of that river and the Bug, being in Russian hands, a fortress had been in building since 1779. This fortress, known as Kherson, and the town which sprung up on the site of the village where it stood, were completed under Potemkin. In the Crimea an even greater fortress and port were planned. Shortly after the annexation a survey of the coast had been ordered, mainly with a view to the erection of defences. It is said that the selection of the bay of Aktier, with its tiny town, in the extreme south-west corner of the peninsula, was made by Catherine herself. It may well be one of those cases in which she took what the experts had told her and made it her own. The transformation of the bay into a port, and the building of the fortress town proceeded apace. Here Potemkin had the services of Rear-Admiral Mackenzie, a Scotsman who, like his fellows Greig and Elphinstone, had been long in service in the Russian navy; and Colonel Upton, a military expert. But ranking above either was the naval architect and engineer, Sir Samuel Bentham, who had already been in Russia for two or three years; and now came to superintend the new works of harbour and fortress that were, in 1784, to be given by Catherine's express command the name compounded from the Russian version of the words augustus and polis, which resolved itself into Sevastopol. There, while this great work was rising on its foundations, Sir Samuel received a visit from his more famous brother, Jeremy, who, while enjoying many conversations with Potemkin—the enjoyment is said to have been mutual—wrote the greater part of his *Defence of Usury* and planned his *Panopticon*.

The naval experts, who included Greig, had more to do than to superintend the construction of fortresses and harbours at Kherson and Sevastopol. The building of battleships was also proceeded with, and keels were laid down at both places.

All this in no wise assuaged the anger of the Turks at what had been done and their suspicion and alarm at what might be intended to be done. Neither anger nor alarm had been lessened when Heraclius, the ruler of Georgia, had placed himself and his country under the protection of Russia, an action which the Turks interpreted, not without justification, as a threat to the whole of the Caucasus. Nor were the Turks, whose interests were immediately threatened, the only nation to experience perturbation. The seizure of the Crimea was probably acquiesced in by Europe generally, and in many cases approved, as a necessary course of action for the safety and welfare, particularly the trading welfare, of Russia. The question of further advances, of what had been planned between Catherine and Joseph, was another matter. Europe had once again to consider the situation in the eastern Mediterranean.

In the meantime, while the diplomatic pot was nearly at the boiling-point, Catherine and Potemkin planned the show that was to set the seal on the triumph in the Crimea and to be remembered in history when much else was forgotten. The Empress of Russia would make a triumphal progress to the Crimea; and would take with her, besides the train of ministers, including Bezborodko, nobles and attendants, both the French Ambassador, Ségur, who had taken up his appointment in 1785, and the English envoy, Alleyne Fitzherbert, afterwards Lord St. Helens, who had come to replace Sir James Harris. More than this, Stanislas Augustus had been invited to journey from Poland, and Joseph himself from Austria, to meet the company as they drew near the Black Sea. It was to be at once a political tour, a pleasure trip, and a diplomatic congress. Certain figures, however, who might have been expected to be among those who accompanied Catherine were conspicuously absent. She had wished to have with her the two grandsons, Alexander and Constantine. She had not proposed to invite their parents. For once the Grand-duke Paul and the duchess triumphed over the Empress-mother. It was, they said, impossible for the grandsons to go with her, as both were suffering from a slight attack of smallpox.

New Year's Day of 1787 was spent at the Winter Palace, after which the court went to Tsarskoe Selo, where the final preparations for the journey were made, and whither came Ségur and Fitzherbert. The former, who kept a full diary of all the happenings, found the days before the departure trying, partly on account of various mishaps, which much annoyed Catherine and so those around her: and partly because he had to struggle with his colleague, Fitzherbert, who, always a delicate man prone to melancholy, was sunk in despair at having to leave behind a lady of St. Petersburg upon whom he had set his affections. But at length, on 18 January, fourteen great sleighs, with between one and two hundred lesser sleighs following, left Tsarskoe Selo.

The imperial sleigh, drawn by thirty horses, was sufficiently large to be divided into three compartments. With the Empress were her ladies-in-waiting, her equerries and the Grand-chancellor, a Shuvalov, nephew to Ivan of that name. In the second sleigh were Ségur and Fitzherbert. The remaining sleighs followed close behind and, wrote Ségur, all appeared to bound through the icy air. Daylight at this time of year lasted no more than six hours but as the procession sped on the darkness was illuminated by the blaze of beacons. The halt for sleeping was usually at a house, although sometimes the sleighs may have served as bed-chambers. All went, as Ségur recorded, with exactitude. At six in the morning the Empress rose—she was always an early riser—transacted business and received her travelling companions. The start for the day was made at nine o'clock; at two o'clock came the halt for dinner and at seven in the evening for supper; after which no more travelling was done, but the Empress either worked or called on some of her companions to join in games such as charades or bout rimés, the popular amusements of the day. The food, the wine, the fruit provided, recorded the French Ambassador, left nothing to be desired, but he grumbled at what were, in his opinion, overheated houses, and much disliked the long hours of darkness.

Kiev was reached on 9 February, and here or a little earlier, Potemkin made his appearance. He did not, however, find a lodging in the palace which had been prepared for Catherine. To the astonishment of many, including the French Ambassador, he had chosen to establish himself in the Lavra or monastery by the cathedral, to which Catherine in her youth had paid her visit. Further details aver that instead of wearing uniform Potemkin also chose to appear on several occasions in a loose robe and unshaven. The interest of the episode is in the light it throws upon one aspect of the man. Sir James Harris had remarked earlier upon his fondness for visiting churches. In certain moods he would speak of becoming a monk. The temperament that, from a mundane existence lived to the full, even to excess, swung over with equal violence to the cloister, and then, changing its purpose, swung back again, was commoner in earlier centuries then it was in the eighteenth. But Ségur was right when he summed up this Lithuanian who may, it is sometimes said, have had eastern blood in him and who had identified himself with a Byzantine enterprise, as a mass of contradictions.

The stay at Kiev extended over six weeks, for it was necessary to wait until the ice of the Dnieper broke up, since when the journey was resumed it was to be by galleys. It was not until 1 May that the procession went on its way, in gaily decked vessels with watching and cheering crowds on the river banks. Travel by the great waterways was common in Russia; but nothing, as Ségur drily remarked, could have been less like ordinary travel than this. Potemkin would hardly have needed to import crowds by force to survey the imperial progress; and the tales subsequently told of the simulated villages may reflect nothing more than that the preparations of all kinds that were normally made for the benefit of royalty— even as booths had been set up along the road from St. Petersburg to Moscow when Catherine and her mother had arrived in Russia—were, in this case, unusually elaborate and even exotic.

At Kaniev, six days' journey down the Dnieper from Kiev, Stanislas Augustus was waiting to greet the Empress. Somewhat further on, came the meeting with Joseph who, with his own accompanying ministers and attendants, joined the procession, which proceeded to Kherson. That town was entered under an arch bearing the inscription, not in Russian, but in Greek: the way to Byzantium. In the newly constructed harbour three battleships were launched. All might well have given Joseph food for thought. But Catherine as well as he were now rudely reminded that that way was not yet open by the appearance outside the harbour, in Turkish waters, of a Turkish flotilla. The intention to cross the estuary had to be abandoned. The climax of the journey was, however, at hand. The Perekop was traversed and the Crimea attained. After five days—during which Ségur and Fitzherbert were lodged in the same tent, lived together, as the former wrote, in perfect unity; and wrote for their respective countries reports which were entirely contradictory one of the other—came the state drive to the Theodora of the Greeks, which was Inkerman, and so to survey the harbour of Sevastopol, with forty ships of war lying in the bay. This now fortified harbour was, the Empress of Russia is reported to have said to the Emperor, only two days' sail from Constantinople. Joseph was not pleased. Nevertheless, it is pointed out by his biographers that, as in his earlier visit, Catherine was again able to sway his opinions by the force of her personality, when his judgment would have held him back. That she had revivified his promise of support in any Turkish expedition she undertook there is little doubt.

Returning from the Crimea, the Emperor took his leave. Catherine proceeded towards Moscow. It was intended that the triumph should continue, and at first it was so. At Poltava a splendid show was staged by Potemkin in commemoration of the victory of Peter the Great; at Kharkov, where he left the Empress, he presented her with a rope of pearls and she, with many gifts, gave him also the title of Prince of Tauris. Already, since 1783, the palace identified with that name had been rising in Smolny, to the east of St. Petersburg, an offering, as witnessed the inscription over the entrance, from the Empress to Potemkin in gratitude. The medal struck in commemoration of the journey showed, on one side, the bust of Potemkin—wearing Roman armour; on the other, a map of the route followed.

At Orel another ceremony was arranged and swords were presented to the leading personages in the train of the Empress. But the brightness of the day was passing and clouds were on the horizon. The huge extent of Russia, the lack of organization and co-ordination, rendered the country peculiarly vulnerable to catastrophe by disease or famine. In this case it was famine. The harvests of the previous year had not been good. As the Empress and her retinue moved north—it was now July—evidence of shortage of grain and consequently of bread was everywhere. Worse than this, reports were received that the prospects for the coming harvest were very bad indeed. Catherine reached Moscow to find the city in the grip of famine prices and part, at least, of the populace on the verge of starvation. Celebrations which had been planned to take place in the Kremlin were abandoned. The imperial procession moved on to reach Tsarskoe Selo on 22 July.

Chapter Nine

Turkey and Poland Again

THE French Ambassador had been of the opinion that the progress to the Crimea had been intended by Potemkin to quicken Catherine's desire to spread her conquests further —in the direction of Constantinople. But even had she not been contemplating a further period for preparation, the famine may well have forced on her the conviction that the moment for a military onslaught was not yet. Challenged the Turks, however, she had. An envoy had been sent to Constantinople to demand that the action of the ruler of Georgia should be endorsed by the cession of that country to Russia; that Bessarabia should likewise be handed over; and that Russia should be permitted to establish hereditary governors in Wallachia and Moldavia.

These demands were, for the Turks, the culminating threat in a series of attacks upon their empire by Russia under Catherine; a series in which there stood out first and foremost the provisions of Kuchuk-Kainardji; then the seizure of the Crimea, followed by the imperial journey, the symbolism of which the Turks were fully able to interpret; the question of Georgia;

and, not least, the presence of Russian agents through the Moslem realm, even in Egypt. Turkey believed the time for action had come. In recent years that country had been experiencing one of their periodic revivals in strength under a vigorous sultan, revivals which had so often had a disconcerting effect upon Europe. Even as Catherine had neared St. Petersburg the Sultan Abdul Hamid had, on 15 July (26 July, N.S.), 1787, informed the Russian envoy in Constantinople that the Russian consuls in Jassy, in Bucharest and in Alexandria must be recalled; that Heraclius of Georgia must again become a vassal of Turkey; that the Turks must have right of search over all Russian ships on the Black Sea. Three weeks later a manifesto to the Turkish people had added the annexation of the Crimea must be avenged and the peninsula restored to Turkey. In those three weeks war had been decided upon. On 5 August (13 August, N.S.) the Russian envoy had been summoned into the presence of the Grand Vizier and thence removed to the prison of the Seven Towers. On 12 September (23 September, N.S.) a manifesto announcing a state of war with Turkey was read in the Russian churches.

Whether or no the Turks were thus wise in forcing events was the subject of much controversy among diplomatists at the time; and among diplomatic historians later. They would have to carry on the fight alone. True, the old order in France

195

still stood for the traditional policy of support of
the Porte; and, in St. Petersburg, Ségur never
ceased to urge upon Catherine—she was fond of
the French Ambassador and would take a good
deal from him—that the fall of the empire she
called barbaric, an adjective the use of which in
that connection he did not dispute, would disinte-
grate all Europe. But the year was 1787. The old
order in France was about to disappear for ever;
and the government whom Ségur represented was
in no position to do anything except to keep a
certain number of officers and a few men in
Constantinople. A contemporary pamphlet accus-
ing the Turks of lack of military judgment
pointed out that they, even if successful, could
never reach St. Petersburg, whereas Russia had
but to win two battles and then would appear in
Constantinople. On the other hand that Turkey
should have acted thus promptly shook the Russian
authorities. That Catherine herself was perturbed
was undeniable. A Russian diarist recorded that
when the manifesto was read on 12 September she
was seen to weep. But he added that the immediate cause of her tears was the absence of Potemkin,
upon whose advice, he said, she had depended for
thirteen years. She had no fear of the outcome of
the struggle, for she was confident of victory.
What she had wished was postponement.

Potemkin was in the south, where he was in
command of one of the two Russian armies, and
with Potemkin was Suvorov.

The first event was a disaster to the Russian fleet which had been built at Sevastopol. In the third week of September, having come out of harbour, at the command of Potemkin, to seek and engage the Turkish fleet, it was scattered and in part destroyed by a terrible gale, one vessel falling into the hands of the Turks. Potemkin was once more true to himself as a man of moods. He who had urged on war in a kind of intoxication now wrote to Catherine in deep depression, and even referred to the possible necessity, since protection by water had gone, for evacuating the Crimea. To which Catherine, as cool in pressing forward, now that the die was cast, as she had been in holding back, bringing her own energy to bear on the despondent general, replied with exhortations to rouse himself and proceed with the campaign. Even as the first letters passed from one to the other, the campaign was proceeding. Within a week of the catastrophe to the Russian fleet the Turks had struck at Kinburn.

At Kinburn was Suvorov, who, since August, had been looking to the defences of that frontier fortress. The skill with which he allowed the Turks to land on the promontory from small boats, protected by the Turkish fleet, and invest the fortress; the desperate triple bayonet charge of his men, aided by Cossack horsemen who harassed the enemy from without; the final destruction of the Turkish army; became a matter of history.

Catherine was overjoyed, as she might well be. The guard to the Crimea held. Now the Turks must be attacked in their own Turkish waters and in their own formidable frontier fortress of Ozchakov, which commanded the estuary of the Bug and the Dnieper from the west. Once, for a short time, Ozchakov had been in Russian hands, when, in 1738, it had fallen to assault; only to be evacuated and restored to Turkey by treaty the following year.

The attack could not be made at once and in the interval the correspondence between the Empress and Potemkin shows him, as Brückner points out, again and again sinking into lethargy. He chose, it was said, to spend most of his time studying the works of Fleury, the French historian and divine who had been confessor to Louis XV —Potemkin's library ultimately formed the basis of the library of the University of Kazan. However sympathetic to the pursuit of reading, Catherine had once more to urge her lieutenant to action; and, presently Potemkin, whether deservedly or not, recovered much of his standing when early in June, 1788, the restored Russian fleet was victorious over the Turkish fleet in the waters off Ozchakov. As July drew to a close, all was ready for the assault on the fortress. It proved to be a long-drawn-out assault, interspersed on the Russian side by bitter and often violent disputes between Potemkin and Suvorov, always antagonistic one to the other. The Turkish forces held out until 6 December (17 December N.S.) when the fortress fell at last amid scenes of fearful carnage. Suvorov had now been removed and Potemkin had the honours of the victory; Catherine among other rewards invested him with the Grand Order of St. George, always coveted and heretofore denied him.

In the meantime Joseph of Austria, true to his promise, had in February, 1788, declared war on Turkey. An Austrian army, not as well equipped as it might have been, had advanced with some slight success into Bosnia. During the next year further advances were made: and siege laid to Belgrade. In this year of 1789 Abdul Hamid died. The war, however, continued. A Russian army had some successes on the line of the river Pruth. Potemkin besieged and took the fortress of Akkerman at the mouth of the Dniester. The outstanding event was the fall to Russia of Ismail on the northern bank of the Danube; which was followed by the seizure of the little coastal fortress called Hadchibei.

All seemed to be going well for Russia, and for her ally. Yet the successes could hardly be described as sweeping. Progress had been very slow and had not been quickened by the want of agreement between the Russian and Austrian generals. Moreover, Russia had had to direct part of her forces elsewhere, to the north, to meet invasion from Sweden.

Gustavus III, King of Sweden, nephew through

his mother of Frederick the Great, ambitious, vigorous and restless, had, since his accession in 1772, been determined to restore the glories of his country. Now, seeing Russia embroiled with Turkey, he believed that the moment had come to avenge the humiliation that Sweden had suffered at the hands of Peter the Great. The early summer of 1788 had seen a sharp interchange of notes between the two countries. Gustavus had asked for Finland and Karelia to be handed over to Sweden; coupling with this the demand that the Crimea should be given back to Turkey. On the rejection of his notes, the Swedish king ordered an attack on Russia by land and by sea, towards Finland to the north and along the Baltic coastline to the south. During 1789 these attacks had been held; at the cost of weakening the Russian front against Turkey. When in the spring of 1790, the Swedish fleet, in spite of a reverse off Revel, drew near to Cronstadt and the roar of the cannon could be heard in St. Petersburg, there was something like a panic in the capital. At one juncture Bezborodko was reported to be in tears. Catherine on the other hand announced that she was finding great consolation in reading Plutarch. But salvation was at hand. Penetrating too far into one of the inlets of the Russian coastline, the Swedish fleet allowed itself to be completely hemmed in by the Russian fleet; and in the sea fight which followed suffered an overwhelming loss in both ships and men. St. Petersburg was saved.

Gustavus, who now had Denmark, the hereditary enemy of Sweden, stirred up by Catherine, on his flank, saw his objects could not be attained and was ready for peace. So, her gaze fixed elsewhere, was Catherine. On 3 August (14 August, N.S.), 1790, a treaty was signed at Verela which left the position as it was before hostilities had commenced.

The war begun by Sweden had thus in one sense been entirely indecisive. But Russia's efforts in the south-east had been hampered and before the treaty with Gustavus had been signed the alliance with Austria had been shattered by death. Joseph II had died on 10 February, having, as he himself said bitterly on his death-bed, failed in all he had tried to do. To Catherine he had been consistently true; and it was to his fidelity to her that his family circle attributed most of his misfortunes. His brother and successor Leopold had no intention of treading the same path. Austria did little or nothing more against Turkey, although it was not until August, 1791, that the two countries concluded a peace that gave nothing to either side.

In the meantime events elsewhere in Europe were having their repercussions on Russia and the Russian-Turkish war.

Catherine had laid the blame for the onslaught on Russia by Sweden not so much upon the shoulders of the Swedish king as upon those of William Pitt, now in his seventh year as Prime

Minister of England. "As Mr. Pitt," she said,
"wishes to chase me from St. Petersburg, I hope
he will allow me to take refuge in Constantinople."
This latter was the last thing desired by Pitt.
The belief of the Empress that he had incited
Sweden to move against her, was, it was generally
agreed, without any foundation. Gustavus had
required no stimulus other than his own ambition.
But Catherine was not in error in seeing in Pitt
an opponent to her principal plan.

Hitherto the attitude of England to the advance
of Russia towards the eastern end of the
Mediterranean and Constantinople had been that
expressed earlier by William Pitt the elder,
reinforced by the growing feeling that the Turks
were a race of decadent barbarians who had no
place in Europe. But Chatham's son was looking
at the matter from another angle. He had reached
the conclusion that the occupation of Constantinople by Russia; that country's further advance into
the Mediterranean; should either or both these
things come about, might well be prejudicial to the
political and commercial interests of England. At
the same time Pitt was inclined towards an alliance
with Prussia, an alliance strongly urged by Sir
James Harris, now ambassador at The Hague, as a
counterpoise to France and to French policy,
which threatened the independence of Holland.
Prussia, on her side, where Frederick William had,
in 1786, succeeded Frederick the Great, was
resentful of the way in which Catherine had

transferred her friendship from Prussia to Austria, and had no liking for the coming together of the latter country and Russia. When therefore, in 1788 Pitt for England and the Foreign Minister Hertsberg for Prussia had concluded the Triple Alliance to which the United Provinces were the third party, both had had in mind the necessity of putting some check upon the ambitions of Russia and Austria, although the primary object of the alliance had been the safety of the third ad-herent. Prussia cherished an additional hope. Her king and minister were determined, if possible, to obtain for their country the towns of Thorn and Dantzig which had been denied to Frederick the Great. For this aim Pitt had no sympathy. He had no wish to see Prussia aggrandized. Nor, as he had told Hertsberg bluntly in 1790, did he wish to precipitate war with Russia; much less a general European war. His object was rather to act with Prussia in hindering Russia's advance without the break which would, all else apart, damage English trade. Ambassadors from England in St. Peters-burg had, over years, been instructed to impress upon the imperial circle the advisability, particu-larly with regard to naval and commercial interests, of friendship with the country they represented.

Catherine, however, was of the opinion that England needed Russia rather than the reverse. The opposition of Pitt was to the great enterprise upon which her heart had for years been set.

She was aware that in his opposition the Prime
Minister had the support of the King of England—
the view taken by George III of Catherine's
probable fidelity was that which had been expressed
by Frederick the Great; and the royal anger when
Harris, on her instructions, had put forward a
request for the Garter for Potemkin was said to
have been unbridled. But the Empress of Russia
had also long been aware that in Pitt's opponent,
Charles Fox, was one who was ready to support
Russia against Turkey, and to use the issue as a
cudgel wherewith to belabour his adversary.
When, in 1788, the king had his second attack of
insanity, the hopes of Catherine and of Fox had
risen high. George had recovered and those hopes
had been dashed. But what came now to be known
as the eastern question was being more and more
looked upon as an ethical, as well as a political
issue. The expulsion from Europe of the
'Asiatic horde', the savage and inhuman
infidels, as Edmund Burke called them, seemed
to many a moral duty. When, on 29 March,
1791, Pitt moved in the Commons a proposal in
an address to the King, based on a convention,
made at Reichenbach between Prussia and
Austria, now reconciled, that Russia should be
invited to accede to the peace which Austria
was about to conclude with Turkey, and that all
conquests should be restored, he received only
lukewarm approbation from his own side. Nor
was the Prime Minister, who dwelt chiefly upon

the desirability of friendship between England and Prussia, the necessity for the withdrawal of Russia behind the line terminated by the fortress of Ozchakov, and the return of that fortress to Turkey, at his best. With the ministerial majority that had been given him in 1784, he could carry his proposals; but in this debate, no less than in that which followed on 15 April, the force, the distinction, the eloquence, were to be found in the speeches on the other side; the speeches of Coke of Norfolk, of Edmund Burke, above all, of Charles Fox; with their appeal for the disappearance of the Turk from Europe, and, by consequence, for support for Russia. In particular the two great orations of Fox moved Catherine to enthusiasm. She wrote to the Russian ambassador that she wished to have sent out to her the best bust obtainable of that statesman. She proposed, she said, to give it a place between those of Cicero and Demosthenes.

In spite of the satisfaction the report of the debates must have given Catherine, her mind was now nevertheless turned towards peace, although, as she wrote to Potemkin, the prospect was as a stone lying on her heart. England might not be prepared to countenance armed intervention, nor even the sending of a fleet to the Mediterranean. Prussia, on the other hand, was assuming a threatening attitude; had spoken openly of war. And in France, the tide of revolution was rising. When Catherine learned

205

of the flight, in June, of the king and queen from Paris, their capture at Varennes, and the forced return to the capital, she was profoundly shocked. The violent laying of hands on royal personages by a rabble was an offence to her sense of fitness; an action not to be tolerated by an Empress autocrat, from whom all law derived. A few months earlier other news had come from Poland, which caused her intense disquiet. She wanted her hands free. Potemkin was ordered to commence negotiations for peace forthwith. But fate was about to deal her a personal blow.

Throughout the latter part of 1790, and the first months of 1791, Potemkin had chosen to abandon the battlefront for St. Petersburg, where he had withdrawn into inertia; out of which he emerged at intervals to give great entertainments in his Tauride Palace; until, shortly after one such, given on 21 April for his Empress, he, having heard of the successes of one of his rivals, had returned to the fighting line. He and Catherine never saw each other again. In October, travelling in the course of the peace negotiations, through Moldavia, he was suffering from the malaria incident to that region. The fever rose, the result, it was said, of his having in his illness insisted on devouring a whole goose; and he expired by the wayside. His body was taken to Kherson, the town which he had seen rise from its foundations; and there, in the cathedral, his tomb was

eventually placed. Catherine wrote to Grimm:
'My pupil, I may say my idol, the Prince
Potemkin, has died in Moldavia.'

The negotiations were continued by Bezborodko;
and on 29 December (9 January, 1792, N.S.)
the treaty of peace was signed at Jassy. Under
the terms of the agreement, the Russian frontier
was advanced to the river Dniester, with the
fortress of Ozchakov in Russian hands. The
Porte recognized the annexation of the Crimea.
The terms of the treaty of Kuchuk-Kainardji
were endorsed. On the other hand, Turkey
took back Moldavia. It was not an outstanding
triumph for Russia, as had been the earlier
treaty. Nor did it correspond with the grandiose
scheme with which the war had begun. Constantinople, its mosques and its sultan, remained
remote. The kingdom of Dacia, over which
Potemkin was to have reigned, was still the
impalpable dream. Nevertheless, the Russian
frontier had crept forward from river to river;
and on the site of Hadchibei a new fortress was
constructed, with a new town, a seaport springing
up around the fortifications, a town which by
1795 was already known as Odessa, named after
an ancient settlement close by, which in its turn
had taken its name from Odessus in Thrace.

And the frontier was now to be advanced in
another region. Even as the negotiations for the
treaty with Turkey were being conducted,
Catherine was thinking of Poland. Once more the

fate of that country was to be intertwined with the Turkish question; and also to be affected by happenings elsewhere, over which it had no control.

In spite of the partition with loss of territory, Poland had remained after 1772 a considerable state, even though with but a puppet king. For the next sixteen years her history had been uneventful; her policy rigidly subordinated to that of Russia. At the same time there had been no amelioration in the condition of the serfs; and despite Catherine's protection of the Dissendents, a great deal of religious intolerance had continued to make itself felt. Between 1788 and 1791 yet another movement for reform had risen to the surface. The more progressive thinkers were talking in terms of a reconstruction of the Diet; of toleration of social improvements. A wave of enthusiasm swept over the country; and the leaders convinced themselves that the future looked bright, the more so because they were persuaded that Russia had her hands full with Turkey. This they had hoped to turn to their advantage, when towards the end of 1790 they had approached the sultan with a view to a compact, by which Poland, in return for certain concessions, was to be given rights of free trade on the Dniester and on the Black Sea. The sultan, however, had been firm in demanding that the return to be made by Poland should be a declaration of war on Russia; and to this the leaders had been unwilling to consent. They had continued with their own plans.

On 3 May, 1791, the Diet had met, despite the protests of the king, under what, from the point of view of Russia, were to all intents and purposes revolutionary conditions. In the course of the speeches, two subjects were prominent. Serfdom must, it was said, be swept away for ever. The elective kingship must likewise disappear. The present ruler might be allowed to remain undisturbed during his lifetime. On his death the crown was to be offered once more to the ruler of Saxony, to pass henceforth from father to son. During the impassioned debates, Stanislas Augustus was himself won over to the cause of the patriots, and it was he who called on the Bishop of Cracow to administer the oath to all present.

In England, Burke, who had applauded the action of Russia against the ' destructive savages ' who were the Turks, but who had also, twenty years earlier, condemned the first partition of Poland, uttered his eulogy of an event which he described as embodying probably the purest good ever conferred on mankind. In Prussia, the news of what had happened was on the whole received with approval. Frederick William had quite sound reasons for thinking that a moderately strong independent buffer state between his own country and Russia would not be amiss. When, in 1785, Ségur had stopped in Berlin

on his way to St. Petersburg, that diplomatist
had been impressed by a remark made to him
by Prince Henry of Prussia. It referred to a
judgment of Diderot. The philosopher, said the
prince, had pointed out that Russia was a
colossus with feet of clay; but an immense colossus,
that could not be attacked because it was
covered with a buckler of ice, and, having very
long arms, might one day be fatal to Germany.
The possibility was never lost sight of by Prussia.

But Catherine, with no thought but determination to crush at once this new and dangerous
movement, which seemed to promise independence for Poland, had no intention of coming
into conflict with Prussia. Her policy was to
win over Frederick William, and this she
succeeded in doing. After all, there were spoils
to be had.

The end was never really in doubt. Poland
stood alone. England, whatever many in the
country might feel, neither could, nor would,
send a fleet to the Baltic or the Black Sea, the
only possible method of giving assistance.
Frederick William came to terms with Catherine,
and even had he not done so, his concern
was now, like that of the Emperor, Leopold,
with the events that were tumbling over one
another in France, and in particular, with the
position of the king and queen. Throughout
1792, when the allied army of Prussia and
Austria crossed the Rhine to restore, as they

believed, the Bourbon monarchy; when Louis was a prisoner in the Temple; when Danton ordered the September massacres; Catherine, partly by diplomacy, partly by troops, steadily proceeded with the crushing of the reformers and reform in Poland. To Grimm, an exile from Paris in Gotha, his poverty relieved by generous help from Catherine, the latter wrote—always seeking, consciously or unconsciously, to justify her actions to others, and to herself—that it was not reform she was fighting in Poland, but Jacobinism. It was a telling argument. That word was already associated in men's minds with all that was extreme in revolution.

The Polish patriot leaders were no match for Catherine in diplomacy. Nor could their troops withstand hers. In spite of the valiant fighting of a little force, in whose ranks Thaddeus Kosciuszko, a young Pole who had fought in the American War of Independence, was conspicuous, the Russian army entered Warsaw with little difficulty.

In August and September, 1793, a Diet sitting at Gradno gave its consent, under duress, to a second partition of the country. Russia took further and extensive slices of territory in Lithuania and White Russia, including part of the Polish area of the Ukraine. To Prussia, as a reward for the acquiescence of its king, fell Dantzig and Thorn, with other territory. But, as before, Russia secured far more than mere territorial gains. The Diet was forced to make other concessions. They agreed that Polish troops should, if asked for, be placed at the disposal of Russia. They agreed to make no treaty with any power except with Russia's consent. They agreed that their government should always be approved by Russia.

Fox was among those who were shocked at this second ruthless cutting up of the unhappy Poland. But he had already fallen from his high estate in Catherine's eyes. His speeches in praise of the revolution in France were, to her, unforgivable. His bust was removed from the gallery in Tsarskoe Selo, where it had been placed.

Poland was a yet more truncated country than before; yet more under the control of Russia; her king—Stanislas had kept his throne —yet more of a puppet king. But she was still a country. To the patriot party, the situation was intolerable. They rushed on their fate. In March 1794, Kosciuszko, with a splendid gesture, raised his standard in Cracow. His special appeal had been to the peasants, to whom he had promised freedom from bondage; and many of them flocked to join his limited forces. A Russian army, taken by surprise, was defeated. This was sufficient to alarm Frederick William, shaken by the events of the preceding year of terror in France, and he immediately offered Catherine assistance. Both sent armies into

Poland. The Prussian army took Cracow, but retreated from before Warsaw, to which they had laid siege. In the meantime, the Russian troops, one of the armies being led by Suvorov, swept forward. In a desperate battle Kosciuszko was wounded and made prisoner. Suvorov's army went on to Warsaw. The fall of the capital, which was followed by an appalling massacre, was the end for Poland. On 3 January, 1795, that country disappeared as a political entity, by the terms of what was to be known as the Third Partition. Russia took the long-coveted Duchy of Courland, with what was left, after the two former partitions, of Lithuania, as well as Vilna. Prussia secured Warsaw and the surrounding district. To Austria, who had not participated in the Second Partition, was given, as a reward for non-interference and a security for the future, Western Galicia, including Cracow and Lublin. Stanislas retired to St. Petersburg. He was given, as a dwelling place in that city, the palace of Gregori Orlov, dead since 1783.

Once more the Russian frontier had moved forward. Yet, quite apart from the ethical aspect of the successive rapes of Poland, profoundly shocking to many, including such men as Charles Fox and Edmund Burke, who had whole-heartedly approved Catherine's exploits against Turkey, there were those who held that she had initially allowed her judgment to be led astray by Frederick when he proposed the first act of partition, and that Nikita Panin was right when he said that a strong, independent Poland, friendly to Russia, and in close touch with her, would be in the best interests of the latter country. Whether these conditions were compatible one with another is dubious. But, having taken the first step, Catherine took the last, and Poland was split up among the three powers.

Chapter Ten

St. Petersburg and its People

IN 1790 a German resident in St. Petersburg, Dr. Johann Gottlieb Georgi, member of the academies of Berlin, of Rome, and of St. Petersburg, published a volume which he entitled *A Description of St. Petersburg*. It was a detailed description, with a generous allowance of statistics; and showed the city—buildings, population, and social and economic life—as it had developed since, in 1703, its founder had laid the foundation stone of the fortress, which, like the city itself, was to be named after him, on one of the islands which lay in the estuary of the Neva.

Since Peter had determined, in the well-worn phrase, to open a window to the west, he had chosen what was, as he saw it, the only possible site; the mouth of the river that emptied itself into the gulf of Finland, opening in its turn into the Baltic. That the delta made by the river, a delta with islands, was a swamp, had counted for nothing. Peter's city had risen on piles driven into the marshy ground. It had been built by forced labour, and at the cost of the lives of thousands of those who had laboured. And from the marshes thus covered unhealthy mists still rose. Despite the marshes, despite the fact that, in that northern latitude, the river was icebound from November to March, or even April, while the shortest day afforded only five and a half hours daylight, despite the terrible floods which inundated the city, when, after south-westerly winds had piled up the waters at the mouth of the estuary, the Neva, as not infrequently occurred, broke its banks, the city stood, a monument to its founder. And, to what Peter had built, his successors had added, notably his daughter Elizabeth, and after her, Catherine, until, in the last decade of the eighteenth century, St. Petersburg was seen as a city of glitter, of opulence and luxury, of art and elegance. If this aspect of the whole overshadowed what was more utilitarian and not only this, but also what was dire poverty, it did not do away with either. They were there, as much a part of St. Petersburg, as was its brilliance.

The utilitarian side had been emphasized in the very foundation of the city. Peter had intended to create a centre for trade as much as a new centre for his government. His foresight was amply justified by the number of ships which in the days of his successors were sailing from and arriving at the quays on the riverside. According to Georgi, the number of those arriving had risen from between one and two

hundred in the years before 1750, to between
nine hundred and a thousand in 1788. The rise,
however, had not been steady. In some years,
notably between 1761 and 1764, there had been
retrogression, to be followed by a leap forward.
But, seen over the whole period, the figures
testified to a steady increase in the trade with
the west; particularly with England, and with
Holland, and extending, during the later years,
to America, although the figure for the ships
arriving from the latter country was, as might
have been expected, the lowest in the table.

Of all the buildings on the banks of the river,
with its ships passing up and down, the Admiralty
was foremost in recalling Peter's original purpose.
It had grown in 1790 from Peter's simple ship-
yard, to a great stone edifice, which was a chancellery; a magazine; a workshop, and by which,
close at hand, was the yard from which the
warships were launched.

The fortress and cathedral of St. Peter and
St. Paul stood on one of the smallest of the
islands. A little distance away was the small
house, built in the Dutch style, from which Peter
had watched the construction of his city.

Thrice the spire of the cathedral had been
destroyed by the lightning which accompanied
the terrible storms that so often visited the
region. It was Catherine under whom a new
spire was erected after the third time of destruction; and this new spire was covered by

217

copper and gilt; and it was she who replaced the clock, destroyed with the spire, by a Dutch chiming clock.

The island on which fortress, cathedral and cottage stood was connected by one of the many bridges of boats with what had been known from the days of Peter, and continued to be known, as the Admiralty quarter, on the left bank of the river, divided, in Catherine's days, into three sections.

To the right of the Admiralty stood the Winter Palace; with its rococo front, its fifteen hundred rooms, its gardens and its pavilions; a monument to the art of Rastrelli; the residence of the rulers of Russia. In her bedroom in that building, which she had ordered to be built, but which she had not lived to see finished, Elizabeth had died. To that building, still incomplete, Catherine had come, with her procession of guards, after the pronouncement in the Church of Our Lady of Kazan.

But, when, in 1790, Georgi was describing the city, the Winter Palace, as designed by the Italian architect, had not only been perfected, but had received notable additions, the conception of Catherine. She had desired to have, over and above the royal apartments, a further set of rooms of a more private character. In 1765, therefore, the French architect, Vallin de la Mothe, designed for her what was called, after its purpose, the Pavillon de Hermitage. In these rooms throughout her reign she read, she worked, she talked with Grimm on his two visits to St. Petersburg, with Diderot on his, with the Englishman Harris, and the Frenchman Ségur, with Orlov, and with Potemkin. But this retreat was not destined to stand alone. About 1775, Velton, a Russian, was commissioned to draw plans for an additional building in which to house the pictures and the many objects of art which Catherine had been steadily adding to the lesser collections made by her predecessors. This new building was connected with the pavilion by an arched bridge which was a corridor. To it, again, was added, about 1780, a theatre, designed, in its turn, by the Italian, Quarenghi. In that theatre were played, on occasions, more than one comedy written by Catherine herself, others by Ségur, who wielded an elegant and witty pen.

The Frenchman, the Russian, the Italian had, between them, over a space of some twenty-five years, created a group of buildings which was one of the glories of Catherine's reign and which, largely reconstructed some sixty years after her death, this time by a German architect, was to continue to be one of the glories of St. Petersburg. Theatre and galleries took their name from the original pavilion. In the event it was the galleries, with their superb collection of pictures, and of precious objects of all kinds, with which the name came to be especially associated.

For the enrichment of those galleries, Catherine

looked for the most part outside Russia; and above all, to Paris, that centre for the connoisseurs and collectors with whom she entered into rivalry. Grimm and Diderot, as well as others, were not infrequently asked to act as her agents; to make a purchase on her behalf, or to set an artist or sculptor to work for her. It was Grimm who bought for her the sculptor Houdon's seated figure of Voltaire, a copy of the figure in the Comédie Française. But one of Catherine's greatest triumphs in Paris was over that ardent collector, Horace Walpole, when she, the slay-czar, or—another of his many names for her—'Empress Gertrude', entered into competition with him in the matter of a purchase, and defeated him. In the summer of 1771, Walpole was in Paris, looking at antiques, attending sales, bespeaking chairs and cabinets and all manner of bibelots for his friends in England, who often thus enlisted his good services. In the market were the pictures of Crozat, Baron de Thiers. These, or some of them, Walpole was determined to secure, even though, as he wrote to England, his financial ruin were to result. But, he added, there had been some dispute on the subject with the Empress of Russia, who had made a bid for the whole collection. Catherine triumphed and the Crozat collection came, the following year, to the galleries in the Hermitage.

It was seven years later that Walpole suffered

even greater annoyance and humiliation at Catherine's hands. In 1779 his nephew George Walpole, of whom neither the uncle nor anyone else had much good to say, decided to sell the pictures at Houghton House, mainly to meet his own and his father's debts. In any case, the proceeding would have grieved the uncle, for the sake, as he wrote to Sir Horace Mann, of the memory of his own father, so closely associated with the collection, as well as on account of the pictures themselves. His resentment was doubled when he learned that the Empress of Russia was negotiating through Mouschkin-Pouschkin, Russian minister plenipotentiary in London, for the purchase of the entire collection. The negotiations were protracted, but in the end, the pictures went to Catherine for a sum said variously to be either £36,000 or £44,500. It was some slight alleviation to Walpole to be able to maintain that the Empress had given a price above their proper value. But, he wrote, he wished that, if they had to be sold at all, they could have gone to the crown of England, instead of that of Russia, where they would certainly be burnt in a wooden palace in the next insurrection. Walpole never quite gave up the idea of an insurrection that would destroy Catherine, any more than he ever quite kept pace with the advance of Russia; and there were, indeed, still many wooden buildings, great and small, alongside the newer erections in stone; for wood was more easily come by in that country of forests than stone, which always had to be brought from a distance.

One other picture at least went from England to the Hermitage Galleries; not as part of a purchased collection, but as a specially commissioned piece. Catherine asked Sir Joshua Reynolds for a painting, giving him liberty of choice of a subject, and making no stipulation as to price. The picture arrived in St. Petersburg in 1790, one of the artist's last works, for in that year his eyesight began to fail. The subject chosen was a representation of the infant Hercules strangling the serpents, intended as an allegory of the young Russia surmounting her difficulties. Sir Joshua had judged well. He could hardly have chosen to transmute into paint an idea, or the treatment of it, which would have been more satisfying to Catherine. With the picture were sent two sets of the *Discourses*, in English and in French. Catherine, conveying her thanks for picture and books through her ambassador in London, bade the latter tell Sir Joshua that she was reading the *Discourses* with avidity, and found in them, as in the picture, the most elevated genius possible. To the fee which had been named, 1500 guineas, she added a gold snuff-box with a portrait of herself in the lid, encircled with diamonds.

The Hermitage buildings, in their triple aspect, represented something of the many-sidedness of the Empress. In the open space or square to the left of the Admiralty another expression of her mind was, while the Hermitage was in building, taking shape.

Elizabeth, daughter of Peter the Great, had had a statue of her father erected in his own city. Catherine determined there should be yet another. In the choice of an artist Diderot had been consulted; and that philosopher had recommended Etienne Falconnet, a sculptor of Paris who had produced a good deal of work of varying quality. In 1766 Falconnet arrived in St. Petersburg and proceeded to the modelling of the statue, a work which occupied the space of twelve years, during which time letters on many subjects, literary and artistic, passed between him and the Empress. The sculptor also had on his hands a series of quarrels with Russian authorities on art.

Completed and cast in bronze, Peter was shown on horseback, reining in his horse on the brink of a precipice, his face towards the Neva, his outstretched hand seeming to point to the city created by his will. It was a huge piece, and was mounted on a block of granite huge to correspond, brought from across the gulf of Finland. On two sides appeared an inscription, once in Russian, once in Latin: Petro Primo Catherina Secunda. It was an acknowledgment to Peter from the stranger who had raised herself to Peter's throne.

One side of the square in which the statue stood, the side furthest from the river, had been occupied by a church, called the Isaac church, ever since the first small wooden building of that dedication had been set up in the early days of the city. Catherine planned for a cathedral. The work was commenced in 1768. Some twenty years later, when Georgi was writing, it had progressed sufficiently for him to describe the walls of granite, faced with marble of many colours, with jasper, with lapis lazuli, and with porphyry, brought from Finland, from Siberia, and from what were now recognized as the treasure caves for stones and minerals, the Urals. The site, facing the statue which was to be immortalized as the bronze horseman, and, beyond the statue, the Neva, was, wrote Georgi, perfect for a building which Catherine intended should be the greatest of all those of the Orthodox Church. It was not until four years after her death that the whole was fully complete. It stood for eighteen years, and was then destroyed— by fire; and was rebuilt once more.

With the Hermitage and the Isaac Cathedral rose, at Catherine's command, yet other buildings; among them some of which Louis Réau, one time Director of the French Institute in St. Petersburg, which had then become Petrograd, said, when writing of art in Russia, that in them Catherine offered witness and recognizance of her affections. Such was the Tauride Palace.

Such, too, was another palace, of an earlier date, built for Gregori Orlov.

The latter building, long to be known as the Marble Palace, faced the Neva, beyond the Hermitage buildings. The design was by Antonio Rinaldo, on classical lines, following the style of architecture now approved through a great part of Europe, a style which modelled itself on the architecture of Greece and Rome, and which had been greatly stimulated by the discoveries at Pompeii where excavations had begun in 1763, and were exciting all polite scholarly and artistic society. But if the lines of the building—it was a low two-storied erection— were simple and severe, the materials used added richness and colour, and glitter. Georgi describes the roof inlaid with copper, the walls of granite faced with marble, many-coloured marble, according to him, although Réau lays particular stress on the employment of that of a grey hue, brought to St. Petersburg for the first time from a quarry recently opened up in Siberia. Windows, continues Georgi, were all set in gilt frames and the balconies, always a feature of the palaces in St. Petersburg, were likewise gilded. Over the entrance, Catherine, as she was later to do in the case of the Tauride Palace, caused to be placed an inscription. This building, said the Russian words, was a thank-offering. But the erection was not commenced before 1770, and took so many years to complete that Orlov

225

can hardly have seen it finished before his death in 1783. It was Stanislas Augustus who benefited.

Orlov had, however, been given before this another palace, a summer palace, outside St. Petersburg, in the little village of Gatchina, whose river of the same name was celebrated for the trout which appeared on every table of importance in the capital. Here, also the work of Rinaldo, had risen a palace, again of classical design, with its arcade of marble columns—this time marble from Finland—standing amid gardens laid out after the English style of the day. This palace, too, with its contents, Catherine took back on Orlov's death, to give it as a residence to her son. It was a convenient spot, where his activities could be supervised; and yet a little remote from the capital.

Thirty miles out of St. Petersburg, and twelve distant from Tsarskoe Selo, Gatchina was one of the many palaces which, with lesser country houses and villas, all with their parks or gardens, were to be found to the south of the capital, and westward by the gulf of Finland. Many, as travellers noted, were at this time newly built, or rebuilt.

The Empress had led the way. Some of the finest architectural work accomplished for her was that to be found in the palaces outside St. Petersburg. Among much else, Quarenghi added the so-called English palace to Peterhof. At Tsarskoe Selo he later designed the Alexander

Palace for Catherine's grandson. But the architect whose genius found its fullest expression in these buildings was Charles Cameron. Réau says that Catherine, growing ever more classically-minded in architecture, found that Rinaldo's style was not sufficiently pure. Therefore, she turned to the Scottish architect, of whom she wrote in a letter, dated August 1779, to Grimm, that he was a great master of design, nourished on antiquities. It was just seven years before this that Cameron had published, in London, his volume on the *Baths of the Romans and their Restoration by Palladio*, to which he had added a preface on *Roman Art*. Amid the work he accomplished in Russia, including some at the Winter Palace, some as far afield as in the Crimea, the building of a new palace at Pavlousk, three miles from Tsarskoe Selo, as a residence for the Grand-duke Paul and his wife, that at Tsarskoe Selo itself was to stand out. There he built for Catherine the arcaded gallery which was to be reckoned the greatest monument to his genius; and the agate pavilion with its three rooms having walls of jasper. And in the palace he decorated Catherine's private apartments, some of them after the Pompeiian style, and designed furniture for the rooms he had decorated.

The parks and gardens, with their formal borders and equally formal clumps of bushes and trees, their pavilions and temples and statuary, were in accordance with the classical lines of the palaces which stood in their midst; and, as elsewhere in Europe, as much attention was given to the gardens as to the buildings. Gardeners were not infrequently brought from England, and Capability Brown had at least one St. Petersburg correspondent in Gould, who laid out the gardens round the Tauride Palace. Either he or another Englishman had laid out the gardens round Potemkin's southern home. During the seventeen-seventies the head of a celebrated nursery garden at Hackney was working at Tsarskoe Selo. His name was John Bush, sometimes spelled Busch, and he may have been of German origin; he is known to have spoken German fluently. His fame extended beyond his own lifetime, for, in later years, his skill was greatly praised by that eminent authority on gardening, James Loudon. Bush had apparently been brought over for some particular piece of work, but when he returned to England, his son remained as one of the imperial gardeners in St. Petersburg.

The palaces, the country houses, and the villas standing thus outside of the capital were really part of it, extensions of that imperial city, to which the owners resorted for change of scene, especially in the spring and summer, seasons whose charm, in those northern latitudes, where spring could come in twenty-four hours and the long summer day knew no night, was all the greater because of contrast with the winter cold and darkness. There were many gardens, too, within the city; gardens round the palaces, gardens round the lesser, but still important, houses and public gardens, all as attractively laid out, in their degree, as those outside the capital.

The public garden known as the Summer Garden, on the bank of the Neva, beyond the Marble Palace, the centre of the outdoor life of St. Petersburg, had been planned by Peter the Great, who had had a small house for himself set up in one corner. A lesser Summer Garden, also with a small palace attached, had been laid out by the Empress Anne. Catherine, always said to be genuinely interested in horticulture, established, in 1785, the first botanical garden in the city, and later added a medical garden, for both of which good works she was later much praised by Loudon.

Many pictures have been drawn of the life led in the capital by that part of society of which the court was the centre—entertainments, the theatre, the music, all on the most sumptuous scale. The splendour of the court banquets and receptions, the gold and silver, the crystal and the porcelain which ornamented the rooms and tables, as well as the luxurious food set forth on the tables, became a by-word in Europe. Sir James Harris, writing to England in January, 1778, said that he had been prepared for magnificence, but that which he had found exceeded all expectation.

It was the Winter Palace which primarily was the scene of the court entertainments, at least in the winter. The rooms in the Hermitage were for Catherine's more intimate gatherings. In the summer Tsarskoe Selo and Peterhof, with their parks and gardens, were an amazing background for the glitter and the richness of the uniforms worn by the men and the dresses worn by the ladies.

For the theatre—the chief building was the new theatre, of stone, standing in the second Admiralty quarter and replacing the first wooden building which had stood in the Summer Garden—there were two official companies, one Russian and one French; besides several free, or non-official companies. The Russian company was made up of twelve actors, of whom the most celebrated was Dnitrewski, and six actresses. The recognized opera company was Italian. The players were mainly of that nationality, but included a few Russians, and, while the majority of the operas played were either French or German, the appearance of several which were the work of native composers marks the birth of the true Russian opera. So also with the dancing company which was part of the opera company. Set dances or ballets, the place of whose origin was France, were performed by French exponents of the art. But some Russians were also to be found in the company, and that, too, may well be regarded as the starting-point of what was later to burgeon so grandly.

That Catherine herself was unmusical did not imply the neglect of music. Court concerts were given frequently. One orchestra was especially attached to the court, others performed in the theatres and, during the summer, in the open air, particularly in the Summer Garden, often in the evening. Music, as well as performers, came for the most part from Italy, from France, and from Germany. But one orchestra was Russian. It was the orchestra of Russian horns, playing what Georgi called the royal hunt music; and had been founded in 1751, under the particular patronage of Elizabeth. This music may perhaps be compared with such a piece as the Messe de St. Hubert, the French hunting music, and was doubtless based on the ancient hunting calls of the forest. But other music was also played by the orchestra, which, however, in Catherine's time, seems to have lost something of its popularity, most of its performances being given in Moscow.

The personal life of nobles and gentry was, as far as exteriors were concerned, rich, even sumptuous. The clothes worn were superb. Georgi gives a list of factories, imperial state factories as well as private establishments, which manufactured fine brocades, silks, and satins; all of which were frequently interwoven with patterns of gold and silver thread. Similar material came from France and from Italy; while English cloth of the finest texture also arrived in bales at the quays. For the making up of their dresses the court ladies and those of allied circles took their fashions from Paris. Not much difference would perhaps have been perceived between the cut of the fine clothes worn at the Winter Palace, and those to be seen at Versailles. But the emeralds, the rubies, the sable and the black fox of Russia spoke of the east in its gorgeousness, rather than of the more restrained west. And as was truly said, the men and women of Russia looked far more Russian in their winter out-door attire—the cloaks, the furs—than at any other time.

The jewels and the furs of the Empress herself were celebrated throughout Europe; and distinguished visitors received at her court spoke of the grandeur of her attire. Yet that grandeur was, it would seem, largely kept for important occasions. Many of those who saw her apart from festivities commented on her fondness for appearing in the long loose garment, a coat held by girdle and buttons, with wide sleeves, that was the typical Russian coat. Ségur, who said that the costume was like that worn by the ' early Muscovites,' added that Catherine donned it to disguise the corpulency of age which, he pointed out, effaces every charm in a woman. Catherine was undoubtedly stout in middle age. She may well have worn the dress for its comfort—there is some evidence that throughout, not only in her clothes, she preferred simplicity and ease in private life. But it was also remarked that the Princess Daschkov followed the fashion set by her imperial mistress, with the suggestion that both were being deliberately Russian, or, as Ségur would have put it, Muscovite. For whatever reason Catherine donned the coat, she liked it well enough to allow herself to be shown in it in more than one of her portraits.

The tables of the nobility and gentry were, like their clothes, luxurious; and like their clothes, were by no means dependent on native produce. The produce of northern Russia, or, rather, that part of northern Russia in which the capital lay, provided the staple foods of sea and river fish; of cabbages, cucumbers, turnips, and radishes, which grew freely in the district, otherwise not propitious for vegetables, together with milk and eggs and butter, coming mostly from certain dairy colonies near St. Petersburg; and bread made both of rye and of wheat. But in addition to the last Georgi gave a list of seven bakers in St. Petersburg who supplied kalatches, the rolls which supposedly could only be made with the water of the Moskva River, said to have been brought from Moscow to St. Petersburg regularly for the purpose. All round the capital, wild berries, particularly, in their respective seasons, wood strawberries, and cranberries, were abundant.

But the very wealthy, like the court, had

much with which to augment their fare. The gardeners who worked in the great gardens in and near St. Petersburg were responsible for fine fruit and fine vegetables grown under glass. It is said, and this is to some extent confirmed by both Georgi and Loudon, that the use of glass for forcing was introduced into Russia by Catherine. Hence, as the reign continued, pineapples, peaches, and nectarines were all added to the native fruits for the tables of the rich; and for these tables again sweets were manufactured by confectioners who had learnt their art in Paris. From France and from Germany came wines to supplement the native vodka and beer.

All these foods and drinks were served for high occasions on gold and silver and the finest porcelain; brought from Augsburg and Nuremberg; from Dresden and Sèvres; but much of both also coming from the native factories of which Georgi gives a list.

Georgi, however, even bowing as he did before the imperial lady and her imperial city, did not fail to note that the life for which the palaces and other great houses were the background represented only one aspect of life in that city. There was also that of which the ships passing up and down the Neva were an integral part.

Along the quays on the riverside, towards its mouth were the shipyards and warehouses—the consummation of the dream of Peter the Great—

of a great trading capital. Behind the Admiralty
and the dwellings on either side stretching
southward, away from the river, was the busy,
active quarter which spoke of commerce. Through
this quarter ran the Nevsky Prospect, with its
two companion streets; all three cut by the
architect Le Blond for Peter, and all radiating
towards the Admiralty. Other principal and
lesser streets also ran towards the river; and all
were intersected by others, at right angles; so that
Georgi was not the only one who commented
on the danger to traffic of such sharp turnings.

Trade and commerce in Russia had indeed,
with some inevitable setbacks, been steadily
increasing since the city had first risen from its
foundations. The figures, and he gives them
lavishly, set down by Georgi, in addition to
those given for the ships, are impressive.

A prosperous trade implied a prosperous
trading folk. And this was so. Complementary
to the commercial quarters were the houses and
villas of the merchants and the upper class of
tradesmen. Ségur spoke of the solid wealth of
these classes, wealth he found amazing. Georgi
commented on the high degree of comfort in
which they lived. A German traveller, C.
Reinbeck, who published, in 1805, a series of
letters describing his travels in Russia, including
reminiscences of the last years of Catherine,
whom he had often seen, was in his turn as
emphatic in his recognition of merchant pros-

perity. Their houses were not palaces, but with the gardens attached were extremely comfortable residences. Their tables, all the commentators agreed, were well spread. Their clothes were good, and often rich. It is probable, and it is indeed implied by various writers that the villas, their contents, and the food found on the table were more truly representative of Russia than were the palaces and the tables of the nobility, in that they owed less to imports from the west, and more to the native wealth of their own country. Nevertheless, since the merchants were themselves the importers, much of what was brought in doubtless found a place in their homes. In the matter of clothes, however, Reinbeck had no doubts. The merchants, he wrote, kept to the costumes of their forefathers, a statement which is probably true also of the professional classes, at least of such as those as did not appear at court. Over their shirts, often embroidered and worn loose over breeches, the men wore the wide-sleeved coat. Their fur hats for the winter might be either helmet-shaped, or low with a brim. One change, however, was already beginning to be remarked. Whereas formerly, and including the early years of Catherine, those who wore this national dress, wore also the traditional Russian high boots, it was observed that in the seventeen-eighties many, except for the winter, were taking to the new low shoes, worn with stockings. Always there was, of course, the transitional state between old customs and new, with now one, and then the other triumphing. One old custom continued, in spite of efforts at abolition. Seventy-odd years before the publication of Georgi's book, Peter the Great had endeavoured, by edict, to make all his people give up their beards, which he regarded as being oriental, and quite unworthy of a folk looking west. This was one of the instances in which his success had been far from complete. During Catherine's reign a number of the upper classes, many of the middle classes, and probably most of the poor, were still wearing beards. But, noted Georgi, such as did were now considered to be somewhat old-fashioned in their outlook.

The wives and daughters of the merchants had, for their part, no reason to be ashamed of their attire. Reinbeck found the older women wearing the fine Russian brocaded jackets, of the old fashion, over their skirts, with lace caps that were worked with pearls. They wore, too, other jewels, set in fine gold and silver work. The younger women indulged in more modern touches which included fine white lawn petticoats, and as fine white lace jackets. In the winter, for young and old women alike, there was the loose coat. And if those worn by the Empress were of brocade and velvet and trimmed with fur, so were those of the wives and daughters of her merchants. Reinbeck saw and admired their fine velvet coats lined with sable.

Georgi wrote of these merchants as a free people, fulfilling their functions in commerce, including sea traffic, under rules laid down by the government. They were a class of whose importance Catherine was fully aware. But they remained, perhaps by their own choice, a class apart. The antagonism between them and the landowners, so evident during the sitting of the commission, continued.

Of the lesser folk, those who described the Russia of Catherine agreed that the more prosperous of the workmen were well off, living in their degree both as regards housing and food—what was placed on the table was good, says Georgi, and was always accompanied by vodka—as comfortably as did the merchant class, and enjoying, not only the public entertainments, in the shape of the illuminations and so forth, so lavishly provided by the crown on all great occasions, but also, pleasures, particularly music and dancing, of a style that was truly national. Of this folk music, music played on instruments of which the balalaika was one, and the folk-dancing, with the concomitant games, Georgi gives a full account.

But below these well-to-do workers, in gradations, were others, of whom the lowest orders, even according to the standards of the eighteenth century, lived in misery indeed. Georgi speaks of their wretched houses, consisting of one room, which might or might not be divided by some planks, and having outside a small yard; the miserable quality of their clothing—a long coat of linen—or of leather, with a sheep's skin thrown over for warmth in the winter; and their equally wretched diet. These people, he said, ate broken meats and fish when they were fortunate; usually they subsisted on hard beans, cucumbers, and a species of sour-milk cheese, poor in quantity as well as in quality. In his opinion, there was every excuse for men and women living thus to fall back as they did on the drink which was cheap, whether it were beer or rough wine or coarse vodka. The drinking houses, which were more often than not drinking cellars, were always full of customers.

Finally, there was the great tribe of servant folk, in the palaces, in the greater houses, working in the gardens, some free and living and lodging well, some half free, some who were serfs, pure and simple.

The marked division of classes had its effect upon the corporate consciousness, or lack thereof, of the capital. This again was accentuated by a more subtle influence. For many the capital was merely a dwelling place for part of the year. This did not so much apply, as might have been expected, to the court, and with the court the court circles and the officials, but rather to others of the gentry class, the merchants and to a large extent the labouring classes. Behind this lay the story of how, in the first instance, the population

239

of St. Petersburg had come to be there at all.

Even as Peter the Great had built a city by force, so he had populated it by force, and force had been required. Sir Bernard Pares, writing his history of Russia, has pointed out that the new city rising from the unhealthy marshes had little or nothing to offer the Russian whose deepest instinct, whatever his status in society, was based on tradition, and that tradition deriving from Moscow.

But, as always, Peter had had his way. In 1710, he had moved the court and the government departments to his new city. In the same year, and during succeeding years, a series of edicts had compelled the migrations thither of a specified number of noble families; of merchants and traders and artisans, all of whom had been required to build themselves houses. And always there had been the inflow of forced labour. This compulsion had bitten deep into the consciousness of all, from the highest to the lowest. But whereas, after one return to Moscow for a short period after Peter's death, the court and government had not only accepted the situation, but had made the capital truly their capital, glorified by the architects employed by the sovereigns, and by those sovereigns again made the centre of a glittering social life, it was otherwise with the more conservative element among the lesser gentry and the merchants. Reinbeck pointed out that the dwellers in Moscow were nearer to the old Russia than were their fellows in St. Petersburg, where the influence of the west was always seeping in. To that he added that his experience informed him that the older capital was the favourite place of residence for all the wealthy who were not definitely attached to the court. In this he included the upper merchant class. Many well-to-do men, he said, merely kept apartments in St. Petersburg, and had their own palace or substantial house in Moscow. This is endorsed by Georgi, who said that a very large proportion of merchants, at least, were only periodical inhabitants of St. Petersburg. They would come to the city for a few months, and then remove themselves, not, as did the court, to the district of palaces and great houses that was really part of St. Petersburg, but going either to Moscow or some country district further afield. This state of affairs, particularly in the case of the merchants and others engaged in trade, was not entirely due to the unpopularity of St. Petersburg. During the winter months the freezing of both sea and river, put an end to sea trade.

The climate had its repercussions upon the labouring class also. They were perforce mobile, coming, or more often being brought into the city, when the spring broke the bonds of winter, and returning to their villages, some six months later, when winter resumed its grip again. It was, said Georgi, this constant movement which

241

made it so difficult for anyone like himself, who approached the business in a scientific spirit, and with a passion for statistics, to estimate truly what was the actual population of St. Petersburg at any given time. But, as he added, general deductions can be made.

In 1789, one of the regular censuses had been taken by the police. The result had given the total number of dwellers in the city, men, women and children, of all classes, and including nationalities other than Russian, as just under 218,000 persons. The figure shows to what degree the population had risen during the past forty years. The first census mentioned by Georgi had been taken in 1750; and the total was then no more than a little over 74,000 persons. In this earlier census, however, no children were included. This must have made a considerable difference. Also, although the register, from the details supplied, appeared on the whole to be well done, the salient fact in estimating its accuracy was the time of year, with the consequent presence or absence of many of the inhabitants, in which the figures were actually taken.

Taking the census of 1789 as it stood, some estimate was made by Georgi of the numbers relating to the various classes found within the city.

Of the entire population something like one-fifth was accounted for by the military establishments; the various regiments, the cadet and other training schools; the wives and children of military persons. This high ratio of the military class to all others might have been expected. All accounts illustrate the important part played by the military at the court, and in the general social life of the capital.

Men of the navy, whose number naturally constantly fluctuated, were reckoned as 10,000 odd at the moment when the census was taken.

The remainder of nearly 163,000 persons was made up of civilians of all classes, gentry, officials, merchants, tradesmen, artisans, and labourers; together with the clergy, and something like 5,000 boys and girls in educational establishments.

The details of this census reveal, as is amply illustrated elsewhere, the number of persons of foreign birth resident in St. Petersburg; another complication in the social development of the city. Here distinctions must be drawn. There were those who had come to St. Petersburg, as elsewhere in Russia, to become as time went on, and often very quickly, completely Russianized; considered as natives, and frequently, as was the case with the minister Panin, as well as others, given a Russian title. At the other end of the scale were such men as Bush the gardener, or Falconnet the sculptor, who came, or who were brought for a particular purpose, to remain only a few years, or less, and then to return to their own country. In between was a great

243

crowd whose status was really indeterminate, many of them holding important positions, and more or less resident, yet keeping their own nationality.

Without making a strict delineation of these various classes of foreigners, Georgi reckoned that those whom he called strangers accounted, in the years in which he was drawing up his guide-book, for as many as one-sixth of the inhabitants of St. Petersburg.

Of these strangers by far the greater number were those of German birth. The preponderance of Germans dated, so said the writer, from the very first days of the city. Then many Germans had arrived, from Moscow and from other cities in Russia, and from Germany itself. The encouragement of this immigration had been part of Peter's deliberate policy. Thereafter had been a supplementary flow from Germany into Russia, and particularly into the capital. These Germans had at all times tended to form themselves into colonies, either in the city, or in country districts. Under Catherine, who is said to have encouraged, if not originated them, several flourishing agricultural German colonies were to be found in the district adjacent to St. Petersburg. They it was who largely supplied the city with its dairy produce.

Next in number to the Germans were men from the British Isles, men of all sorts and conditions. Among them was included the important group or colony of merchants, who had their own, officially recognized, business houses, and place on the quays. At all times a considerable number, both of English and Scots, were to be found in the service of the Russian Admiralty; from men like the admirals, Greig and Elphinstone, and the naval engineer Sir Samuel Bentham, down to ordinary seamen and naval workers of all kinds. English and Scots were likewise well represented in the professions and trades, apart from those who, like Cameron, have left famous names. The engraver James Walker, a pupil of Valentine Green, came to St. Petersburg in 1784, to remain at least twenty years, and to make some well-known drawings of the Empress, and of members of her court. Among others mentioned by Georgi was Jackson, an Englishman who made musical instruments, and Morgan, who sold, and may also have made, mathematical instruments. There was at least one English tailor, who specialized in riding clothes.

Pre-eminent, however, perhaps among the English and Scots, not only in the capital, but elsewhere in Russia, were the gardeners, Bush and Gould, and others, who laid out so many of the great gardens around the palaces; and above all, the medical men and the apothecaries.

Peter had favoured the immigration of Dutch workers and their families no less than he had favoured that of Germans; and during his time a large number of Dutch had settled in St. Petersburg. This immigration had, however, considerably slowed down, or had even stopped. In 1789, far fewer names of Dutch residents were to be found on the lists than would have been the case in earlier years. It is difficult to say whether many of the earlier immigrants had left Russia to return to their own country, or whether they had become, in the course of time, Russianized.

Extensive colonization was typical of the Germans in Russia; partial colonization was not infrequent among the Dutch, and to a certain extent, the English, although in the latter instance the numbers of individuals working for themselves was very great. Among the French and the Italians was little or no colonization. Men of these nationalities appear as individuals, and almost entirely in relation to the arts. Among the architects the names of Rinaldo and Quarenghi stood out as that of Rastrelli had done earlier. The names of others, if not as eminent as these, at least names of distinction, with a lesser group, are to be found among the musicians—the leader of the imperial choir was more often than not an Italian—the actors and the painters. And at least one well-known Austrian was for long resident in St. Petersburg. This was a woman. She was Nanette Mahueu, the celebrated riding mistress, and teacher of what in her native town of Vienna had been elevated into an art.

Lastly came those nationalities drawn from the provinces which lay to the east and south of Russia, and from Asia. Armenians were to be found in the capital; chiefly employed in the jewellery trade, but also as shopmen generally, and as attendants in bathing establishments. Tartars, Kalmucks, and Moors were also mentioned, mainly in menial positions. But in numbers they were comparatively few, nor were the Armenians really numerous. Here was another marked distinction between St. Petersburg and Moscow, and yet more between St. Petersburg and cities lying to the east and to the south-east. In Moscow were to be found many more men who were racially either completely eastern, or who belonged more to the east than to the west. In such a city as Kazan the balance was entirely in favour of the east. 'At last', wrote Catherine to Voltaire, when she visited that city in the spring of 1767, 'I am in Asia'. But St. Petersburg was a city which looked westward.

Chapter Eleven

The Arts and the Sciences

ON the Vasili Ostrov or Basil Island, the triangular piece of land enisled by the streams of the Great and the Little Neva, with its base washed by the Gulf of Finland, stood two buildings which, each in its degree, represented an important side of Russian life. The one was the academy of Science; the other the academy of Fine Arts.

The latter had originally been a department of the former, added in 1755 by the Empress Elizabeth, almost certainly at the instigation of Peter Shuvalov. In 1764 Catherine separated this department from the parent body, and bestowed upon it the dignity of a separate college, with its own statutes. For what was in effect a new foundation, she decreed a new building. The site selected faced that arm of the river which was called the Great Neva. The plans were drawn up by Vallin de la Mothe. Associated with the Frenchman and largely responsible for the construction of what was one of the most beautiful buildings in the city was the Russian architect, Kokorinov.

The work was commenced in 1765. Georgi,

looking at the edifice in 1788, when it was nearly finished, described it as a three-storied building, standing alone, with a court before, and surrounded by gardens, among which could be discerned some wooden houses. The front, with its severe lines and colonnades, was modelled on the French classical form.

The function of the new academy was to undertake a general supervision of all the branches of art throughout Russia; to foster and care for these, and to provide instruction in them. The classes for the latter purpose included painting in all its aspects; etching and engraving, architecture, fine gold and silver work, and lastly, the making of specialized mechanical instruments of all kinds.

In these and cognate subjects regular courses were provided for paying pupils. But the statutes also required the admittance every three years of sixty boys of six years of age. These boys were to be given, at the expense of the academy, first a good general education, and then instruction in one or more of the arts. At fourteen years of age they were to sit for an examination, the result of which gave the successful candidates travelling scholarships for the study of some branch of art.

The teachers in the academy were at first largely foreigners, with Frenchmen perhaps predominating. But the impetus given to the study of art had much to do with the rise during the century of a native school of painters. The most prominent was probably Levitski, who portrayed the Empress, her court, and the chief personalities of the day. The most interesting in his personal history was Shibanov. A serf of Potemkin, he was never technically given his freedom. None the less, he was a recognized and admired portrait painter. His best-known picture of Catherine was sent to Kiev. But his work included more than the portraits of the great, which, interesting and valuable in themselves, were produced at the time in St. Petersburg, as elsewhere in Europe, in profusion. He painted also pictures of peasant life; a departure to be set beside the growing fashion for depicting landscape. It was these men, Levitski, Shibanov, and others, who re-created native art after the long hiatus since the days when the expression of that art, to which Byzantine influence had much to say, had been in murals and ikons; to the glory of which the Vladimir ikon in the chapel of the Assumption in Moscow, the Kazan virgin in its church in St. Petersburg, and many another treasure bore witness.

Architecture was another study in the academy. Here, however, a truly native school was slower in making its way than was the case with painting. Réau always declared that it needed the invasion of Napoleon to make the school of Russian architecture really effective. But against this must be set the subtle influence of Russia upon the architects from Italy, from France, and from Scotland, who produced their great designs for her. It was to be noted that, whether the building was baroque or rococo or classical, or, for the first years after the death of Catherine, empire, in each and every case the style was somehow or somewhere Russianized.

The other sections of the academy, less important in themselves than those in which painting and architecture were studied, nevertheless reveal the lively interest taken in handicraft of all kinds, particularly in gold and metal work and the making of instruments of all kinds.

This academy of Fine Arts was, however, in one sense subsidiary to its fellow college on the island. The academy of Science, from which the former had sprung, had been the foundation of Peter the Great. For that academy, in the last year of his life, statutes had been drawn up at his request by Leibnitz. The building was opened in the following year by Peter's widow and successor, Catherine.

The scheme, as conceived by Peter, and as carried out, included a gymnasium with a professoriate for the instruction of students. The statutes show the clear intention that the college itself was not only to be a centre of learning for the capital, but that its function, resembling that of its subsidiary, was also to be to supervise and to encourage all branches of learning throughout Russia. The institution was of the

more importance because the university of
Moscow, was, when founded in 1757 by
Elizabeth, not only the earliest university in
Russia, but remained the only one until the
early years of the nineteenth century.

The academy owed much to the fostering care
of Elizabeth. And, in her reign, the institution
had at least one remarkable student in Michael
Lomonosov. That son of a peasant had made his
way, by his own energy and gifts, to Moscow, to
Germany; and then to the academy in St.
Petersburg, to become eminent not only in history
and literature, but in the sciences. To what
Elizabeth had done, her successor added. That
from the first the institution had been under the
direct patronage of the reigning sovereign was,
given the social structure of Russia generally,
and of St. Petersburg in particular, probably
highly advantageous to the institution. Given
Catherine's tastes and temperament, the arrangement was also most acceptable to her.

As supreme patron the monarch nominated the
president of the academy. The danger was that
this might imply that the president would be an
honorary figure, more important at the court
than in the academy itself. This may well have
been true of one of Catherine's early nominees
for the office, Waldimir Orlov. On the other
hand, that family were known to be interested in
learning. When, however, in 1783, the Empress
put in as president her friend the Princess

Daschkov, the former was probably doing more service to the academy, and to learning in Russia in general, than seemed at the first sight likely. The lady who was Horace Walpole's 'virago' and Frederick the Great's 'buzzing fly' had a real appreciation and knowledge of learning. And, over and above this, the instructions given her by the royal patron were of great significance. They marked Catherine's comprehension of what was evident everywhere, the quickening growth of national feeling. The commands to the new president were definite. The latter was as far as possible to forward the study of Russian, and to insist on the use of the Russian tongue in the classes and in all the transactions of the college.

Something was accomplished. Georgi, drawing up lists of learned works, approved the production of a new comprehensive Russian grammar; and, significant indeed, after all that had happened, an entirely new Russian atlas. Of the sixty-six writers, some novelists, but mainly literary and scientific authors, whom Georgi considered worthy of mention, a considerable number have Russian names. Lomonosov died before Catherine had been very long on the throne. But after him, writing in Russian as he had done, came Karamzin. The great work of the latter, however, the *History of the Russian State*, in which, as has been said, he discovered Russia to the Russians, belongs not to the reign of Catherine, but to that of her grandson. While thus encouraging the study and use of the native language, Catherine appointed, in 1768, a special commission to supervise translations of foreign works. She herself, at various times, rendered some of the plays of Shakespeare into Russian.

All these facts, seen in conjunction with the number of both booksellers and printers which Georgi gives as flourishing in St. Petersburg during the latter years of the reign, reveal a vigorous intellectual life within the city, owing much to foreign sources, but one in which a native literature was pushing its way to the light.

Schools in the capital, over and beyond the gymnasium attached to the academy, in particular military schools for the sons of officers and for other boys intending to follow a military career, had received an impetus when Peter the Great had decreed compulsory education for the upper classes as a part of their obligations to the state. This particular obligation had been unpopular and was often evaded. But as interest in culture, not as an obligation, but for its own sake, had progressed, so had the schools. Catherine appears to have founded at least one new cadet school. Her most famous foundation was not, however, for boys, but for girls. In 1772, she sent to Voltaire for his inspection a draft of the rules she proposed for a school for young ladies after the model of the school founded by Madame de

Maintenon at St. Cyr. The sage replied in terms of modified approval. The establishment might, he thought, produce a battalion of amazons. To that Catherine in her turn replied that the intention was neither to turn the young ladies into amazons, nor yet into an order of religious. Their education, she wrote, was to be designed to make them neither prudes nor yet coquettes; but rather to fit them to be the delight of any family. A home for the school was provided at Smolny, on the eastern outskirts of St. Petersburg, the corner made by the bend of the Neva as it turned to the west and to the sea. There the palace was to be built for Potemkin, Prince of Tauris. There already stood the convent in which Elizabeth had proposed to end her days, built around the five-domed cathedral dedicated to the Resurrection, convent and cathedral alike designed by Rastrelli. Now, adjacent to the rococo building which many held to be Rastrelli's masterpiece, Catherine added another, to shelter her young ladies. The school was to remain the most celebrated institution of its kind in St. Petersburg, under the particular patronage of the sovereign.

All boys and girls of the upper classes were not, however, sent to schools, whether day or boarding schools. Georgi mentions the many learned tutors engaged to teach in families. Such men played a considerable part in the social life, and many of them, although their standing varied much, were foreigners of distinction, men who in themselves provided a channel for foreign influence.

That influence was also felt in the custom, long since approved by Peter the Great, of sending boys and young men to western Europe for educational purposes. In 1767, the Princess Daschkov herself, not yet president of the academy, had taken her son to England to place him in Westminster School. Thence, in 1772, she had proceeded with him to Edinburgh, where he had attended the university classes; and the princess, given apartments in the palace of Holyrood by the Duke of Hamilton, had revelled in the learned society of Edinburgh of the seventeen-seventies; the city in which the new town was about to be laid out. At Holyrood the princess held receptions, and wrote in her diary that the very names of some of her guests, Robertson—he was then principal of the university—Stair, Adam Smith and Ferguson, were sufficient to denote the privilege and pleasure she enjoyed in their society. Adam Smith had not yet published his *Wealth of Nations*. But William Robertson's *History of the Reign of Charles V* had appeared in 1769, and had won the warm approval of the royal mistress of the princess, to whom it had been sent. Bearing the sub-title that it was intended as a *View of the Progress of Society from the Subversion of the Roman Empire to the Beginning of the Sixteenth Century*, and recognized as one of the earliest attempts at historical generalization based upon an accumulation of facts, it was the type of work to appeal to Catherine. To the author she wrote that it had become her constant companion and added a substantial token of her approbation in the form of a gold box set with diamonds.

The education of the boys and girls of the upper classes in St. Petersburg was thus well provided for, whether at home or abroad.

Further, Georgi gives details of a number of other schools in St. Petersburg, where children coming from families of a status below those recognized as the upper classes received education. These schools, for boys and for girls, were of several different grades; and some of them, at least, were attended by the children of the poor. For the year 1789 Georgi gives the total number of children in all schools in the capital as 2,607 boys, and 522 girls.

Lastly, in 1785, Catherine founded a royal school of the theatre. Instruction for the pupils, who were to be of Russian nationality, was to include the arts of acting, of music, and of the dance. It was a step towards the expression of the Russian genius for those arts.

All these schools belonged to St. Petersburg, and it is probable, almost certain, that they represented a more advanced system of education than was found elsewhere.

But Moscow had its university and Kiev, with

257

its great traditions, its academy and theological college. It was, moreover, in Moscow that Catherine set up a girls' school seven years before she founded that at Smolny, whose fame was so far to exceed that of its sister school.

There is also evidence that Catherine had plans for a system of education that should extend over the whole country; a principle that had been laid down in the statutes drawn up for the academy. Here, as in so many other matters, Catherine had sought inspiration from what was happening elsewhere. It was in the first half of the seventeen-sixties, those early years of her reign, when she was drawing up her instructions, and calling her assembly to consider the government of Russia, that she had been thinking of education in Russia; and, in 1764, had sent forth a commission to the British Isles, to report on the universities and schools found there, and from the material thus collected, to draw up suggestions for the introduction into Russia of a new system of education.

The survey—comprehensive indeed—covered the universities of Great Britain, the public schools, the endowed and grammar schools; boarding and day schools in country districts, and lastly such charity schools as the chartered schools in Ireland, founded in 1733 by Royal Patent, and what were known as Welsh Circulating Schools.

After the report came the recommendations

for Russia. Beginning on the lowest rung of the ladder, it was suggested that lesser, or primary schools should be set up in villages for the benefit of the poorer class of the inhabitants. In these schools the subjects of instruction were to be chiefly religion and reading, but writing and a very little arithmetic might be added, 'although these may be subject to abuse'. The force of the latter remark is seen in the additional recommendation that it was primarily necessary to accustom the children of the poor to industry, to propriety of behaviour, and to great economy.

Schools of the next rank were to be seminaries, gymnasiums and colleges, for the children of all classes of free persons. The curriculum suggested included languages, both living and dead.

Finally, there was to be an extended scheme of universities, academies, military training establishments, and so forth.

No investigation has so far determined to what extent any attempt was made to put any part of the suggested scheme into practice. Catherine, however, was not the only person in her realm who was concerned about education. Some at least of the nobles and gentry thought on the same lines as did their Empress; and even had instructions drawn up for the education of the children of peasants on their estates. Such instructions were not, it is true, as a rule on the generous side. It was usually suggested that the teachers should be the parish clergy, and that the cost should be met by a tax on the residents. Moreover, reminiscent of the report of Catherine's commissioners, these instructions insisted that education must not go too far in the case of the poor. Even an advanced thinker and humanitarian such as Rychkov, a member of the Free Economical Society, thought that only a select number of children should be taught to write, and these taken from the well-to-do peasant class. If, it was said, the peasant learns to write, he will be able to forge a passport. Possible mobility of the peasant worker was a recurrent nightmare, whether the employer owner were the state or a private person.

The opinion of Mr. James Mavor, expressed in his *Economic History of Russia*, is that while it is impossible that any general public system of education obtained in the latter years of Catherine, there nevertheless existed for the poorer classes a number of schools in St. Petersburg, and other towns, to which in many cases landowners sent the children of their dependents; and in the country a certain number of widely scattered peasant schools. There was not, he thinks, anything like complete illiteracy. That at all times an unusually gifted and determined boy could rise, in spite of all drawbacks and hindrances, is shown by the careers of such men as Lomonosov and Shibanov.

In yet another direction Catherine stimulated

the advance of science with considerable success. This was the science of medicine.

Peter the Great had instituted a system of hospitals; considerably expanded by his successor, the Empress Anne. Either at the end of the one reign or the beginning of the other, a medical chancery had been founded. In 1769, Catherine turned this chancery into a college with president and fellows, and statutes which gave it supreme oversight of medical affairs in all Russia. Georgi noted the presence, in Catherine's St. Petersburg, of a considerable number of both surgeons and doctors. He added a not unimpressive list of the then existing hospitals, including a certain number of state institutions for those unable to pay for themselves. Moscow and other towns also had their hospitals. There is also evidence for the existence of a large number of doctors elsewhere than in the capital, including the villages. As might be expected, Russia, particularly in the more remote districts, differed not at all from other countries in having a large number of those who were termed quacks. The inference can be drawn from the accounts of travellers that, as was also the case elsewhere, some of these quacks gave treatment by no means bad in itself, others offered something approaching witchcraft.

But an interesting point was the presence in Russia, from at least the end of the sixteenth century onwards, and continuing throughout the

261

reign of Catherine, of a large number of stranger doctors and among these a high proportion drawn from England and Scotland. Doctor Dee, the doctor son of the astrologer of Elizabeth of England, had been only one among several to practise in Russia during the early seventeenth century. Others had followed in his train, so freely, that by the middle of the next century there was said to be no town of any size within the boundaries of Russia in which a Scots or English doctor, or failing that, an apothecary of either nation, could not be found. These foreigners—many of them settled in Russia and founded families there—were not invariably popular. Ségur had little good to say of Dr. John Rogerson of Dumfries, who, arriving in Russia in 1766, was highly esteemed by Catherine, and was appointed court physician. This gentleman, wrote Ségur sourly, dabbled as much in politics as in medicine, and did pretty well out of both. The last remark appears to have been undeniably true. Rogerson, whose stay in Russia extended over twenty years, and who accompanied the Empress on the progress to the Crimea and received—to Ségur's great annoyance—a sword in commemoration, is known to have returned to Dumfries with sufficient wealth to buy a substantial estate and build himself a fine mansion thereon. More interesting than the coming of Dr. Rogerson to Russia was the arrival there of the Quaker physician, Dr. Thomas Dimsdale; not as an adventurer but especially summoned by the Empress in 1768, in consequence of his reputation in the practice of inoculation for smallpox; on the method of which he had, in 1767, published a treatise.

The smallpox had long taken a terrible toll in Russia. Catherine had a personal fear of the disease, perhaps in consequence of the attack sustained by her husband on the visit to Kiev. That fear was particularly noted on two occasions at least; once when she found one of her personal attendants was a victim and another time when she believed she herself had taken the infection, although the illness proved to be the measles. There is also every reason to believe that she was genuinely concerned with the epidemics which swept the country and genuinely interested in what she had learnt of a new method of overcoming them. So Dr. Dimsdale was brought over, and since example was important the operation was performed in semi-public, in a house on the island where stood the fortress and cathedral of St. Peter and St. Paul. The experiment was viewed with no particular favour by many of those around Catherine and still less by the populace at large. Those who had advocated or had undergone inoculation in its early stages in England and elsewhere had had the same experience. In the case of Dr. Dimsdale, so hostile was said to be the feeling against him in St. Petersburg, partly doubtless induced by the fact of his being a stranger, that Catherine ordered post horses to be ready at any moment in case he should have to flee. But all went well. The Quaker doctor returned to his native Buckinghamshire—by way of Prussia, where he paid a visit to Frederick the Great—enriched by a fee of £10,000 down, an allowance of £2,000 for expenses and an annuity of £500. In addition he was made a councillor of state in Russia with the hereditary title of baron and given the right to a new coat of arms. Coming once more to Russia in 1784 he inoculated, among others, Catherine's two grandsons, who three years later were proclaimed by their parents to be suffering from the disease—in a slight form—when summoned to join their grandmother's progress to the Crimea. By this time the practice of inoculation seems to have spread somewhat and a state hospital, also on an island, to which anyone might resort for the treatment, had been established.

It should be added that the scientist, William Tooke, a Fellow of the Royal Society in England, and a member of the Imperial Academy of Science and of the Free Economical Society in St. Petersburg, resident for many years in Russia, remarked, in his *View of the Russian Empire During the Reign of Catherine II*, which he published in London in 1799, that, in his opinion, some form of inoculation may well have been practised in the further parts of Russia before Catherine's time; introduced from the east where it had certainly been utilized long before Lady Mary Wortley-Montagu, returning from Constantinople in 1721, had cried aloud its virtues.

During the seventeen-seventies another infectious fever even more alarming than the smallpox terrified a great part of Russia. After years of quiescence the plague reappeared. It was recognized that the infection was brought by the soldiers who had served in Turkey. Striking first, as might be expected, on the frontiers, it swept through the villages, destroying in at least one instance all the inhabitants of the place within a few days. Penetrating towards the interior, it reached Moscow; and the spring and summer of 1771 saw one of the most fearful epidemics which that city, inured of old to them, had ever experienced. For some years at least, further outbreaks occurred. They were associated, and probably rightly so, not only with the Turkish war but with Pugachev and his men. They certainly helped to intensify the terror excited in Moscow and the surrounding districts by that rebel and his followers.

What, apart from epidemics, was the general state of health throughout Russia with which Catherine's medical college was expected to cope is, of course, impossible to estimate. William Tooke, for one, declared that, save in one particular, the Russians were more healthy than other nations with which he was acquainted, and gave as the reason for this that both rich and poor trusted very little in doctors, and took but little medicine; while all alike made great use of the sweating or vapour baths. The cynical attitude towards treatment by doctors can be matched anywhere and everywhere. Sir James Harris, while in Russia, had the misfortune on one occasion to be thrown from his coach and to receive wounds in his neck. He wrote to his family that they need feel no anxiety since he had cured himself by pouring brandy and water into the wounds and keeping all surgeons away.

The vapour baths and hot baths always had been, and continued to be, the subject of comment by all travellers. Many agreed with William Tooke that they were valuable for health reasons; but others said that they did not really make for cleanliness in the case of the poor since the Russian of the lower classes obstinately kept to one set of garments—it is likely that many would have only possessed one set—although these were sometimes washed with himself on the occasion of a visit to a bath.

Tooke, however, while approving the baths, disapproved of the habit of drinking to excess, which, he declared, was all too common; and, which, in his opinion, accounted for the high number of deaths among males in middle life, as compared with the exceptionally low rate of mortality among infants, children and adolescents and women of all ages. But against Tooke's account must be set the terrible effects of the famine and fevers which constantly swept the country. Nor do all writers agree with his conclusions.

More scientific exploration for which Catherine may have been directly responsible was the sending forth of expeditions into the furthermost parts of Russia to examine, in Tooke's words, the nature of the inhabitants, the soil, the vegetable and mineral wealth. This practice had already obtained under Peter the Great. Catherine's decision to continue was made, according to Tooke, in 1767. The first party set off in 1768. The leader was Samuel Gmelin, physician, of Tübingen. He was accompanied by four students, an apothecary, a huntsman, a draftsman and an escort of soldiers. Their destination was the Persian frontier. There they remained during four years. Then fate overtook them. They were captured by Persian bandits, and Gmelin, at least, died in prison. His writings were subsequently recovered, although with difficulty. Among his successors several were of his own nationality, including Professor Pallas, who was to advise on the cultivation of the Ukraine. One at least was a Swede—Professor Falk from Upsala—and others were Russian. The district covered ranged from the White Sea to the Caspian. Some of the explorers remained away for six years; none for less than two years. Some, like Gmelin, never returned. Levitz, the astronomer, was seized by Pugachev's men, tortured and killed. Professor

Falk committed suicide. Among those who did return was Johann Georgi himself whose special area was the Ural district, where he collected facts so dear to his heart, on flora, fauna and minerals, not to speak of soil and weather conditions. For obvious reasons, connected with their mineral wealth, the Urals were what they had long been, the chief attraction for exploration. But it was Catherine who first ordered a survey to be made of the Caucasus and Georgia, sending thither in 1768 two German scientists, Doctors Guldenstadt and Reinegg, to report on regions whose history went back two thousand years, to be intermingled with legend and fable.

Chapter Twelve

The Last Years

REINBECK, the German traveller, gave in one of his letters a picture of Catherine as he saw her, during the last years of her life. The chestnut hair was snowy white; and the cheeks much rouged; but the blue eyes were as bright as ever. The corpulency upon which Ségur had remarked ten or twelve years before had now, if anything, increased; and was more noticeable because the figure, which had never been very tall, had now become almost squat. Nevertheless, dignity and grandeur were, as ever, embodied in the bearing, particularly in the poise of the head— the carriage of that head seldom failed to be commented upon. Reinbeck added that he had seen the Empress chiefly in her own apartments, since, at the time when he knew her, she appeared but seldom in public. She was, he said, usually dressed in a loose robe which was a combination of the Oriental and the European, an endorsement of Ségur's earlier description of the garment favoured by the Empress. Reinbeck, with a little more kindness than the Frenchman had displayed, added that the cut was certainly most suitable for a matron's wear.

Here, in her old age, seated in the rooms designed for her in the Hermitage or, as another wrote of her about the same time, slowly pacing the gallery that Cameron had built for her in Tsarskoe Selo, was the woman who had done great things for the country of her adoption. The Greek Empire and the Kingdom of Dacia might still be no more than dreams; but the Black Sea had been reached; and Sevastopol and Odessa were witnesses to that triumphal advance. Catherine was justified when she exclaimed that coming to Russia a dowerless bride, she had provided her own marriage portion in the shape of the Crimea. Eastward and southward had been penetration into the Urals, the Caucasus, Georgia, the uttermost parts of Russia's domains, even beyond, to explore their resources. And on the west, the boundary of the Russian state now ran, by the absorption of Courland, and the policy—whether a wise policy or no—of the partition of Poland, from the mouth of the Niemen on the north to that of the Dniester on the south.

So had the frontiers moved forward. There had been expansion of another kind. Russia, looked on hitherto, even after Peter the Great had opened the window to the west, as interesting, in many respects important, but always remote, was now recognized as having taken her place among the European powers. The views and intentions of St. Petersburg counted for as much, must be as carefully considered, as those of Vienna, of Paris, of Berlin, of London, and herein the position to which the Empress had attained, among her fellow rulers, among the statesmen of Europe, had been a potent factor.

And much had been accomplished within Russia itself. To that, the academies of the Arts and Sciences with their ramifications: the new buildings; the vigorous intellectual life, at least within the two capitals, displaying, amid that which had been transplanted from the west, the strong young growth of a national culture; all alike bore witness.

But for these things a price had to be paid. The cost of the successive wars had been enormous. And to this had to be added the expenditure of the court and all that appertained to its elegant grandeur. The crown mines, the vast crown lands, helped to provide an income for the ruler of Russia beyond the dreams of other crowned heads in Europe. But what was spent out-paced even that income. The full effects of the extravagant spending upon the economic life of the country were felt only after Catherine's day. But already there were underground rumblings of discontent, not solely concerned with serfdom, which spoke of trouble to come. Harris was not the only one who foretold a possible revolution of a kind that, as he wrote to his government at home, might well go to great lengths.

It is vain to speculate whether the achievements of the reign—and they were great achievements

—could have been accomplished otherwise; with more attention paid to their cost, not only in money but in the economic and social factors involved. The question is tied up with that of the vast, the unwieldy, the traditional administrative system of Russia. In fairness to Catherine, it must be remembered that like some of those around her, she was aware of the problems arising out of the flaws in that system. She had drawn up the *Instructions*. She had called her Commission. And next to nothing had happened. There had been the partially successful attempts to alter the provincial administration. There had been a few changes in the composition and working of the senate and the higher departments. But these were far from constituting anything approaching a reform of the government of the country. And the record of the treatment of what Catherine had, in her early years as Empress, recognized as the running sore of the government, serfdom, was grim enough.

One factor making for the increased depression of the position of the serfs derived directly from the 1762 edict. Released from obligatory service, many of the nobles and gentry went to live on their estates, whether large or small—and a number were quite small, little more than farms. But all, save the smallest which could be, and often were, worked by the owner and his family, required labour. Further, yet more workers were needed as the ranks of the serf-owners were

perpetually swelled by newcomers, who, in accordance with the system of grading in the departments, were given the status of gentry, along with
lands. At the same time the reconstruction of the
system of provincial government gave all these
landowners, save the most lowly, more and more
control over local justice and administration.
Many of the changes were based on good principles. But the result for the serf was to make his
master also his magistrate and his policeman.

Then, in 1785, came an edict from Catherine
which recognized the nobility as a separate estate,
having particular rights and privileges. It was not
an isolated edict, nor was it intended to be one
promulgated solely for the advantage of the landowners. It was part of a general policy whereby
Catherine was seeking to develop the idea of
dividing the nation into estates generally. Another
edict of the same year endeavoured, while giving
charters to the more important towns, to create
an estate of merchants and others; an attempt
which was destined to come to very little or
nothing. The position of the merchant remained a
peculiar problem. But the creation of the estate
of nobles did no good to the serfs.

Catherine must also be held responsible, when
Russia advanced southwards, for the introduction
of serfdom into the Ukraine, where it had been
hitherto unknown. And it was she who made
grants of serfs with lands, particularly to her
favourites, on a far greater scale than had been

done previously. It might be said that, given the conditions prevailing in Russia, with agriculture and serfdom tied together, it had been necessary to do these things, particularly in the Ukraine with its rich lands awaiting development and its shortage of labour, until the question of serfdom could be dealt with as a whole. And it is to Catherine's credit that some foreign observers, Ségur among them, were of the opinion that on the whole, at any rate during the first part of the reign, a certain mildness of treatment of serfs was evident and was directly due to the influence of the Empress. The latter did, in fact, issue edicts, among others, which forbade the landowners to inflict savage punishment on their serfs, or to dispose of them by public sale; edicts often evaded.

Nevertheless, throughout, Catherine was capitulating, in greater or less degree, to the difficulties and complexities of the social structure, of which the landowners and serfdom were an integral part. In 1790 came a happening which made evident to what extent that capitulation had gone; what an alteration in disposition—and that not for the better—had occurred in Catherine herself.

There is probably no time when some persons at least are not aware of the moral evils of their epoch. The eighteenth century in Russia was no exception to the rule. There were those who were conscious of the ethical as well as the political problems of serfdom; and the Empress was not the only one in the realm to have read and absorbed the ideas of the philosophers and the humanitarians. Expression of opinion was hardly easy. Yet opinion was expressed. In 1790, a customs house official, Raditschev, published a book which had the seemingly innocent title of *A Journey from St. Petersburg to Moscow.* In truth it contained an outspoken and relentless description of serfdom and its evils. A wave of fury agitated the greater part of the landowning class. What Raditschev had said was unforgivable; and the possible results, in the view of the nobility, appalling. Thus affronted, they carried Catherine with them. Raditschev was sent to Siberia. His own comment on the situation was as true a one as could be made. He had written, he said, just a few years too late. His book held no pronouncement that did not correspond with those made earlier by the Empress.

Raditschev was very right. Catherine in 1790 had travelled a long way from the Empress who had meditated on the evils of serfdom and had drawn up the *Instructions.* The passing of the years had brought about other changes than those noticed in her personal appearance. It would have been a remarkable woman indeed, of great humility of soul, who could have resisted the corroding effects of the absolutism of the Russian crown; of the successes that attended her reign; of the incense offered to her wisdom by the very men coming from whom it was most flattering. And humility of soul did not belong to Catherine.

Since Sir James Harris, on his arrival in St. Petersburg, had written of the deterioration remarked in the character of the Empress, and had assigned reasons for it, none could fail to notice that the process had gathered impetus. Everything to which the English Ambassador had referred—success; flattery; sensuality, expressed in the long line of young lovers—had continued to do its work on the supreme autocrat. And, in particular, two events, one within and one without Russia, contributed to a hardening of Catherine's heart. The first was the rebellion of Pugachev; the other was the French Revolution; the shadow of the last was already well over the horizon when Raditschev produced his book. Each of these events, in its degree, angered the Empress; may have frightened her, though she was not easily frightened. But each— and this may well have been their most significant effect—was also profoundly shocking to her self-esteem as a ruler. Her attitude can be summed up in the remark made by Maurice Baring, that lover of Russia, when he wrote that the one thing that an autocrat, however enlightened, finds difficulty in understanding is a revolution. How should it not be so since the essence of benevolent despotism is that the decisions of its representative are, in his or her own opinion, invariably founded upon wisdom and righteous judgment?

Yet, underneath all, however intertwined with, and overlaid by, other strands of conduct,

276

Catherine's conviction that her métier was to govern, according to the principles in which she continued to the very end to announce her belief, persisted. It was in character that, during the decade before the French revolution, she should have sought to project these principles into the future, when she determined that they should form the basis of the education of the boy whom she almost certainly intended to be her direct successor.

As the years went on, it was noticed that the relations between Catherine and her son did not improve. It appears certain that the situation was greatly aggravated by intrigues of which, during the last years of his life, Nikita Panin was the centre. A good deal of evidence goes to show that Panin played or endeavoured to play, with respect to the young court, precisely the same part that Bestúzhev had played earlier. Panin was no Bestúzhev; and the Grand-duke Paul and his duchess were very far from the stature of the Grand-duchess Catherine. Nevertheless, the latter as Empress had good reason to know what this repetition of history might imply. Paul and his wife were kept at Gatchina, more rigidly in the background than ever and were ever more carefully watched. And history repeated itself in yet another way. The Empress Elizabeth had gradually become aware of the deficiencies of the nephew whom she had chosen to succeed her. Catherine in her turn became aware of the deficiencies of her son. There was, indeed, in Paul so much that recalled Peter III as to justify the conclusion that the two were father and son. It was upon the grand-children that the hopes of the grandmother were set.

The relations of Catherine with the boys Alexander and Constantine were from the first close. That she loved the two as she loved few others there is little doubt. From the earliest days she had sought to win their affection in return; she had picture books made for them; she wrote for them tales of early Russian history; tales which were intended to develop, but did not, into a complete history of Russia. Later when she was away from them as on the progress to the Crimea, or they from her as when the Grand-duke Alexander visited Finland, a constant correspondence was kept up; and Brückner pronounces these letters the most charming of all Catherine ever wrote. And with her love went her plans for the future, a future in which she could not share but which she desired to mould. The influence she exercised on Alexander was great. It was equalled by that of the tutor she chose for him. That choice bridged the gulf between the Catherine of the later years and the young Empress who had worked on the *Instructions*.

Frederick Cæsar la Harpe had distinguished himself as a young man in his native canton of Vaux by the vigour with which he had pressed the claims of that independently minded district

against the overbearing aristocratic autocracy of
the wealthy canton of Berne. So vehemently had
he conducted this opposition that the advisability
of a short absence from his country was suggested
to him. He, a rebel against the established order
and an ardent would-be reformer of that order,
had already made the acquaintance of Grimm.
Through the good offices of the latter he was
appointed in 1782 as tutor to a son of the nobility
in St. Petersburg. It was probably Grimm who
had drawn Catherine's attention to the new
arrival; although the latter was known both to
Catherine and the Grand-duke Paul by repute.

Once he was in St. Petersburg it was certainly
a very short time before the Empress entered into
communication with him and presently desired
him to send her a memoir of his views. The memoir
was sent. It reflected, through the medium of
a lofty and even noble mind, all that la Harpe had
learned from the encyclopædists who had been
Catherine's teachers too; and it included an
exposition of the doctrine inserted in the *Instructions*; that the sovereign exists for the people.
There was some discussion and then la Harpe, the
republican reformer, found himself appointed as
tutor to Catherine's grandsons: to whom, but
particularly to Alexander, he expounded, clearly
with the consent of the Empress, his liberal
theories of government. Yet all did not go quite
smoothly. The eight or nine years over which la
Harpe's stay in St. Petersburg was prolonged

were punctuated by accusations brought against him by those both inside and outside of Russia, who disliked and mistrusted his political ideas. Undoubtedly at one time he was unwise in using his position to interfere, on behalf of his beloved canton of Vaux and her claims, in affairs at home. Catherine gave him sound advice when she told him roundly that that kind of thing, coming from St. Petersburg, would not do. She herself evidently liked him to the end, and seems to have wished for his continued stay in St. Petersburg even after the marriage of his elder pupil. But opposing forces were too much for her. She submitted to the inevitable and allowed the marriage—to a Princess of Baden—to be made the occasion for getting rid of the tutor. La Harpe returned, not to Vaux, but to Geneva to carry on his fight there.

In July, 1796, a third son was born to the Grand-duke Paul and his Grand-duchess. The child, nineteen years younger than his brother Alexander, was baptized as Nicholas.

On 17 December in the same year, Sir James Harris, now Lord Malmesbury and ambassador to the French republic, wrote, at ten o'clock at night, to Canning, then Secretary for Foreign Affairs, a letter in which he said that for some time past a report of the death of the Empress of Russia had been circulated in Paris. To this report he himself had hitherto given no credence, since, he said, the Empress was always getting killed off just about this time of the year. He had, however, now received official confirmation that the statement was correct. Catherine had died a month since.

On 5 November (16 November, N.S.) the Empress had held a small salon in the Hermitage, at which she appeared to be in high spirits, although certain signs of age and failing health had for some time been noticed by those around her. The following day, after granting some interviews, she remained alone in her private room in the Winter Palace. Prolonged silence alarmed the court. The door was broken open and Catherine discovered prone and senseless by her writing table. She never recovered consciousness; and died the next day. A prolonged lying-in-state in the chapel of the palace; and then the body was taken to the cathedral of St. Peter and St. Paul. There, when the long solemn litany with which the Orthodox Church said farewell to its dead was chanted, the coffin was placed in the vault below the floor of the building. It was not placed there alone. With it was lowered into the vault another coffin, on the drapery of which also rested an imperial crown. Paul, proclaimed Emperor at last, had ordered that the coffin of Peter III should be brought from the monastery of St. Alexander Nevski, where it had lain for thirty-four years, to be set, in that funeral ceremony, with that of Catherine—the shadow of Peter beside her at the end.

It was generally believed that a document in

which Catherine had nominated Alexander as her successor had been prepared, and that only the suddenness of the end had saved Paul from exclusion from the throne. Four and a half years later he lay dead on the floor in his bedroom, strangled by the scarf of one of the conspirators who had burst into his chamber at midnight. And Alexander, the enigmatic Alexander, the grandson of Catherine, the pupil of la Harpe, succeeded to the glories and the problems that were Russia. But Alexander left no heir. Constantine, his brother, so far from becoming a Greek Emperor, as his grandmother had planned for him, declined even the Russian crown. The inheritance passed to the third brother, Nicholas, who, at the time of Catherine's death, had been a babe of six months; and through him the line descended.

In February, 1905, one hundred and nine years after the death of Catherine, an exhibition was held in St. Petersburg. The patron was the Emperor, another Nicholas, the great-grandson of the first of that name; the last of his line. The organizer was Serge Diaghilev. The place was the Tauride Palace. The subject was a collection of historic Russian portraits, dating from 1705 to 1905, gathered from all over Russia. An English woman, the wife of Charles Williams, one who, like Maurice Baring, loved Russia, walked through the gilded rooms; looked out from the tall windows set in their elaborate frames. Here, in all the self-confident magnificence of the eighteenth century, was the building that Catherine had caused to be erected for Potemkin; a token of her love, her gratitude, her pride. Here lay the park; the lakes; the pavilions; the gardens for which the advice of Capability Brown had been sought. From the walls of the room devoted to the reign of Catherine, she herself, the ladies of her court, the men who had served her, among them the one-time owner of the Palace, looked down. And there, wrote the visitor, where the Prince of Tauris had so often entertained his Empress, was embodied the farewell of old Russia to the new.

For Further Reading

The literature of the period is vast. This short bibliography is intended merely to suggest certain standard works to the reader as starting-points for further study.

GENERAL:

The relevant chapters in *Cambridge Modern History, volume VI, The Eighteenth Century*; and in Sir Bernard Pares' *History of Russia*. Both volumes contain full bibliographies, to which reference should be made.

BIOGRAPHY:

Alexander Brückner. *Katherine die Zweite.* This is particularly valuable in the use made of original sources and in the footnotes and references.

POLAND:

Cambridge History of Poland, 1697-1935, ed. W. F. Reddaway, etc.

TURKEY:

Albert Sorel. *La question d'Orient au Dix-huitième Siècle.*

DOCUMENTS AND CORRESPONDENCE:

A selection in an English translation from the correspondence between Catherine II and Voltaire has been edited by W. F. Reddaway in the volume called *Documents of Catherine the Great*. This volume contains also the Instructions in the English text of 1768. In his introduction Mr. Reddaway gives his reasons for concluding that the letters to Voltaire were of Catherine's own composition, concerning which queries have arisen. Mr. Reddaway's decision has been accepted in the present volume. Among the other collections of Catherine's letters, to which references are made in the text, may be mentioned, as an example of her early writing, *The Correspondence of Catherine the Great when Grand-duchess, with Sir Charles Hanbury-Williams*, edited by the Earl of Ilchester and Mrs. Langford-Brooke.

PERSONAL MEMOIRS OF CATHERINE:

The authoritative edition is that of A. Herzen (French—English). In the present volume it is assumed that the memoirs are genuine, but they must be read remembering that they represent what Catherine wished to think, and wished others to think, about her actions and character.

SOCIAL AND ECONOMIC:

James Mavor. *The Economic History of Russia.*

ART:

Louis Réau. *L'Art Russe*, vol. ii. The fine photography of Prince Georgis Loukomski's *Charles Cameron* has a particular value when so much of that architect's work has gone for ever. The booklet entitled *Russian Art*, edited by D. Talbot Rice, published for the Exhibition of Russian Art in London, 1935, contains much valuable information in a small space.

DESCRIPTIVE:

Contemporary accounts of life in Russia by Johann Georgi, William Tooke and C. Reinbeck are mentioned in the text. For the story of the city of St. Petersburg there can be recommended Charles Marsden, *Palmyra of the North*. Only the last few pages are, however, devoted to the reign of Catherine. The best novel dealing with the period is A. Pushkin's tale of the rebellion of Pugachev. It has been translated several times into English under the title *The Captain's Daughter*. The latest translation is that of 1915, by T. Keane.

In addition to the above the student may like to know of two articles on the bibliography of Russian History. The first, by Sir Bernard Pares, appeared in *History*, vol. IV (1919), pp. 23-29. The second, by Leo Loewenson, in the same periodical, vol. XXVIII, No. 108, new series, September 1943.

Index

INDEX

INDEX

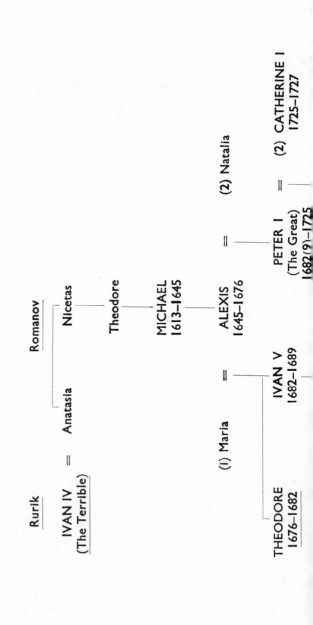

Rurik

IVAN IV = Anatasia
(The Terrible)

Romanov

Nicetas

Theodore

MICHAEL
1613–1645

ALEXIS
1645–1676

(i) Maria = = (2) Natalia

THEODORE
1676–1682

IVAN V
1682–1689

PETER I = (2) CATHERINE I
(The Great)   1725–1727
1682(9)–1725

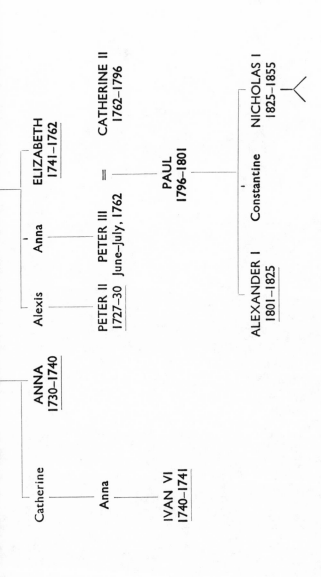

Catherine

ANNA
1730–1740

Anna

IVAN VI
1740–1741

Alexis

Anna

ELIZABETH
1741–1762

PETER II
1727–30

PETER III
June–July, 1762

=

CATHERINE II
1762–1796

PAUL
1796–1801

ALEXANDER I
1801–1825

Constantine

NICHOLAS I
1825–1855